Praise for *Mento...*

"The internet has allowed us to connect to millions of people around the globe. And yet, Christian women say they are lonelier than ever. Ladies, we need each other. *Mentoring for All Seasons* provides excellent biblical insight on how to connect, encourage, motivate, and inspire each other. Janet Thompson uniquely presents practical ideas and steps on how to become, or find, a mentor. With a wide range of topics, and covering the vastly different seasons in a Christian woman's life, *Mentoring for All Seasons* teaches how to find, or be, the mentor Jesus desires. With wisdom, joy, and experience, Janet Thompson guides Christian women though the seasons of life and offers hope and help on the much-needed subject of mentoring."

—**Laura Petherbridge,** speaker, and author of *When "I Do" Becomes "I Don't"*, *The Smart Stepmom, 101 Tips for the Smart Stepmom*, and *Quiet Moments for the Stepmom Soul*

"Janet Thompson's book is informative and thorough, making it a great 'how to' book for those who want a spiritual mentor, those who want to mentor others, and those who direct and coordinate women's ministries. They can find answers to their questions about how to connect and nurture in this book. What I like best, though, are the many real-life stories Janet includes. I appreciate Janet's gathering and sharing numerous stories that illustrate and clarify her message and inspire women to take action."

—**Brenda Poinsett,** Bible teacher, conference speaker, and author of numerous books, including *The Friendship Factor: Why Women Need Other Women* and *He Said What?!: Jesus' Amazing Words to Women*

"*Mentoring for All Seasons* is a handbook for women in all stages of life and relationships. I am the founder of a ministry that is all about equipping women leaders who are passionate to guide teen girls on a rite of passage journey into womanhood. Thus, mentoring is a high focus in this ministry. Therefore, Janet's reference to mentors and their value to girls in their teen years is right on. She stated it well when she wrote, 'sometimes daughters need a mentor more than mom . . . because they think that mom's views aren't objective.' This is a powerful truth! Mentors often validate what mom has been saying all along. Excellent recommendations are made in the Mentor Tips. One tip at the beginning that is very key is having trustworthy, open communication with the mentee's parent(s) as well as with the mentee herself. A great resource! This will be one for my personal library."

—**Doreen Hanna,** founder and president, Treasured Celebrations, author of
  Raising a Modern Day Princess

"Janet takes the scary out of mentoring. She gives step-by-step simple ways to reach out to the next generation with godly wisdom, practical life lessons, and day-to-day applications. No matter what season of life a woman is in, from teens to twilight, Janet's book helps mentors understand typical tender places and common empty spaces. This is one of the most comprehensive books on mentoring I've ever read. Readers will turn the last page and think, *I can do this!*"

—**Sharon Jaynes,** author of 21 books, including *The Power of a Woman's Words*
  and *Take Hold of the Faith You Long For*

"As someone who has been mentored since adolescence by kingdom leaders and now has served as a mentor to many entering the counseling field, I appreciate *Mentoring for All Seasons* tremendously. My favorite chapter is titled 'The Stages of Mentoring.' As a professional counselor, I often find women struggle with figuring out how to go about this process, and Janet does a great job of guiding all of us in building healthy mentoring relationships."

—**Michelle Nietert, MA, LPC-S,** professional speaker, counselor, and author

"Janet Thompson powerfully and purposefully shows women of today how to put the biblical principle of mentoring into a real-life practice. Mentor and mentee practical tips and personal stories are provided to help the reader catch the vision and live it out. As Janet points out, the generation gap is not God's plan. Mentoring closes the divide and unites believers. Spiritual growth happens when we share life and focus on God's faithfulness."

—**Lori Wildenberg,** speaker, author of many books (including *Messy Journey:
  How Grace & Truth Offer the Prodigal a Way Home*), lead mentor mom at
  Moms Together Facebook Community, and co-founder of 1 Corinthians 13
  Parenting—a resource page for ministry leaders and parents

"In a world where mentoring has taken a back seat to social media and remote relationships, Janet Thompson's new book, *Mentoring for All Seasons*, reclaims the power of personal relationships and God's call on our lives to mentor and be mentored. In *Mentoring for All Seasons*, Janet shares the *why, what, where, when,* and *how* of mentoring in such a practical and powerful way that readers will be equipped and emboldened to once again embrace Titus 2 personally, as well as corporately. I highly recommend it as a *must read* for all women and women's ministry leaders alike!"

—**Stephanie Shott,** author, Bible teacher, and founder of The MOM Initiative, an in-reach and outreach missional ministry dedicated to helping the body of Christ minister to moms who know Christ and reach those who don't

"As a fledgling women's ministry leader almost twenty years ago, I was delighted to discover Janet Thompson's *Woman to Woman Mentoring* resources. I read and studied her materials with relish in order to develop the core of my own mentoring ministry. At that time Janet was a lone pioneer for Titus 2 mentoring ministries. She understood the need for intentional spiritual mentoring among women of faith in a practical but also deeply personal way. This work of Janet's will build solid, Bible-focused women's ministry in the church. I can guarantee that! We have to do this, women of God, for the church to not just survive, but thrive."

—**Joneal Kirby, PhD,** director, Heartfelt Ministries, author of *Heartfelt: A Woman's Guide to Creating Meaningful Friendships*

"If you'd like to find a mentor, be a mentor, or launch a mentoring ministry, this is the book you've been looking for! In *Mentoring for All Seasons*, Janet Thomson skillfully addresses the questions you have while presenting a strategic, biblical, in-depth plan for effective mentoring. She includes powerful stories of women in every stage of life and shares real-life examples that reveal how you can follow through on becoming an encourager and an example to the women God places in your life. I highly recommend this resource!"

—**Carol Kent,** speaker, and author of *Becoming a Woman of Influence*

"I am pleased to write an endorsement for Janet Thompson's new book on mentoring. God has blessed my life through precious women who have poured his truth into me in profound ways. At every stage of life, he has taught and encouraged me through wiser women: Beth in high school, Mrs. George in college, JoAnn in seminary, and Dorothy in ministry. I have also walked through life with younger women, especially as the president's wife at New Orleans Baptist Theological Seminary. What a joy to share what God teaches me with others! I am grateful for Janet's most recent book, which presents the mandate, mission, and methods of mentoring in a clear and convicting way. I am eager to use her book as a text in my mentoring classes as well as with younger women I mentor, and highly recommend it to you!"

—**Rhonda H. Kelley, PhD,** adjunct professor of women's ministry, New Orleans Baptist Theological Seminary

"Janet Thompson knows mentoring. She's lived it, breathed it, taught it, and remains as passionate about it today as she was 20 years ago when I met her. In *Mentoring for All Seasons*, she will encourage, inspire, and thoroughly equip you to join her in answering God's call to impact the next generation of women."

—**Cindi McMenamin,** pastor's wife, women's ministry director, and author of several books, including *When Women Walk Alone* and *Drama Free: Finding Peace When Emotions Overwhelm You*

"Everyone needs a mentor, at every age and stage of life! Janet Thompson gives us the inspiration, encouragement, and equipping to be a mentor and find a mentor—no matter what season we are in!"

—**Pam Farrel,** author of 45 books, including *7 Simple Skills™ for Every Woman: Success in Keeping Everything Together*

MENTORING

FOR ALL SEASONS

Sharing
Life Experiences &
God's Faithfulness

JANET THOMPSON

LEAFWOOD
PUBLISHERS
an imprint of Abilene Christian University Press

MENTORING FOR ALL SEASONS

Sharing Life Experiences and God's Faithfulness

LEAFWOOD
P U B L I S H E R S

an imprint of Abilene Christian University Press

Cover design by ThinkPen Design, LLC | Interior text design by Sandy Armstrong

Leafwood Publishers is an imprint of Abilene Christian University Press
ACU Box 29138, Abilene, Texas 79699

1-877-816-4455 | www.leafwoodpublishers.com

17 18 19 20 21 22 / 7 6 5 4 3 2 1

To all the M&M's—past, current, and future—
who have shared life experiences and
God's faithfulness with each other.

CONTENTS

Section One
Christian Mentoring 101

Section Two
Life Seasons of Mentors and Mentees (M&M's)

ACKNOWLEDGMENTS

I stand in awe that God allows me to participate in an amazing mentoring ministry to help women live out his scriptural plan for one generation to teach and train the next generation. I've learned so much from those who have gone before me, and pray I leave a mentoring legacy to those who come behind me.

With more love and gratitude than mere words can adequately express, I applaud these treasured supporters, mentors, encouragers, and prayer partners who inspired *Mentoring for All Seasons: Sharing Life Experiences and God's Faithfulness*:

- *My Lord and Savior, Jesus Christ.* You called a recently rededicated prodigal daughter who knew nothing about mentoring to "Feed my sheep."
- *My loving helpmate hubby, Dave.* You are perfectly suited for me. I could never do all the Lord has asked of me without your love, support, and willingness to step out of your comfort zone—cooking dinners! Thank you for reading, editing, gatekeeping, filling in life's gaps during deadlines, believing in me, and being part of *About His Work* Ministries with me. I love you!
- *Pastors Rick Warren, Brad Sprague, and Doug Slaybaugh.* You championed and supported me in starting Woman to Woman Mentoring Ministry at Saddleback Church—a

ministry God has blessed beyond what any of us could have ever imagined.

- *Chris Adams.* You caught the vision of the Woman to Woman Mentoring Ministry, and thousands of women have enjoyed the blessings of M&M relationships.
- *M&M's.* Many of you shared your amazing stories that made me laugh, pause, cry, and marvel at what God does when two women walk side by side with Jesus in the middle.
- *Sharron Pankhurst.* My sister in Christ and treasured friend, you are always eager to edit another book. I appreciate your tenaciousness, dedication, and encouragement.
- *My church family.* My fellow brothers and sisters in Christ at Crouch Community Church, and especially my friends in Couples Small Group, you have been the saints praying me through this project!
- *Gary Myers.* You always saw the truth and value in the projects we did together. Your legacy lives on through the authors you allowed the privilege of collaborating with Leafwood Publishers. I pray this book will be part of God's revival as one generation accepts the call to mentor the next generation.
- *Duane Anderson.* You saw the vision for this book and worked diligently to ensure the cover portrayed the message. Thank you for always including me in this creative process.
- *Rachel Paul.* You are an editor and project manager full of grace, mercy, kindness, and prayer.
- *Mary Hardegree and the Leafwood Team.* Your support and professional attention to every project we do together blesses me.

PREFACE

When you get where you're going, don't forget to turn around and help the next one in line. Always stay humble and kind.

—Tim McGraw, "Humble and Kind"

I thank God for my spiritual daughters over the years. I never had a mentor, so I feel God gave me a burden to befriend and touch the lives of younger women, as it says in Titus chapter 2.

—Lillian Penner

There is a time for everything,
and a season for every activity under the heavens.

—Ecclesiastes 3:1

The phone rang. I didn't recognize the number, but it was local. I let it ring. I was busy writing this book. My husband answered the phone; it was Melanie calling for me. I knew Melanie from church and our small community but couldn't imagine why she would be calling.

When I came to the phone and Melanie started talking, I wondered if God was testing me. She said God put me on her heart as a published author and fellow sister in Christ, and would I help her with some writing projects?

As I listened to Melanie, my mind raced to the pending book deadline. I was sick with yet another cold, had a full upcoming travel and speaking schedule, had grandchildren's soccer games to attend, and was facing possible eye surgery, and the doctors were still trying to figure out a neurological problem I was having.

As she shared her heart, I prayed, *Really God, now? Maybe when I'm between books, or healthy, or have a few months at home . . . why not have her call me then, when it would be an easy yes?*

He reminded me of the Facebook message two nights prior from a young woman wanting to know how she could speak boldly and confidently without offending, as she had witnessed me do in blogs and on Facebook. Another message, from a woman I met at a speaking engagement, thanked me for mentoring her through my blogs, newsletters, and Facebook posts.

Then there was the Facebook message from Anna, who I'd met on vacation two years ago: "Janet, I'm in a place in life where I'm in desperate need of a Christian woman mentor. My faith walk has been at a standstill for a while . . . years probably. I'm struggling with family, marriage, health . . . do you do any personal mentoring? Or can you recommend where I should turn?"

And there was the email from Lisa B.—a single grandmother raising her prodigal granddaughter who had read my book, *Praying for Your Prodigal Daughter*—asking for prayer, guidance, and encouragement.

In the midst of these rapid-fire thoughts, I heard Melanie say, "I might need to meet with you several times."

> *Lord, please, I can't mentor every woman. And I'm certainly not perfect, as you point out to me daily. Yet you've given me a passion to raise up mentors in the church and community. You continue putting in front of me an unending line of women who need me to share my experiences and your faithfulness through writing, speaking, and one-on-one mentoring so they can go and do the same.*

I felt the Lord prompting me to say yes to Melanie. So I promised to pray and call her back when I felt better. I smiled as I hung up the phone and winked at God. I knew it was *really* God calling me. He has used me to create a mentoring ministry founded on equipping, encouraging, and challenging women to mentor from their experiences, even in the middle of their messes. Now he was challenging *me* to do exactly that. I did! And so can you.

You may already have a heart for mentoring and want to learn more about how to mentor. Or you might be the "Melanie," brave enough to make the phone call or approach the woman you want to mentor you. As Melanie later told me,

> My parents raised me in a Southern Baptist church. The ministers and church body felt a mission calling for all ages to be fully trained and equipped to minister and witness— through Scriptures and prayer life—according to an individual's needs. It was impressed upon the younger in Christ that seasoned Christians *always* were willing to mentor. So it seemed natural to seek your guidance as I further explore writing with specific purpose. I truly appreciate your willingness, and, yes, this will most likely be a process, as "life" will play into our time together.

Melanie preciously expresses the Titus 2 concept I pray *every* church adopts and promotes, because God's plan is for one generation of women to teach and train the next generation.

Whatever season you're in now, you just came out of a season, and you'll soon be going into the next one. Share with another woman what you learned from the past season, and look for a woman who will help you navigate your upcoming season. I pray that *Mentoring for All Seasons* equips you to mentor and seek a mentor. As we go through the seasons of our life, we vacillate between being a mentee and being the mentor—that's the beauty of *Sharing Life Experiences and God's Faithfulness.*

Mentors Are Righteous Oaks

Tracy Steel's letter to her mentor describes being a mentor as a righteous oak. If you're an older woman, I don't think you'll be able to read this without feeling a tug at your heart to walk across the sanctuary and hug a younger woman. If you're the younger woman, look around the sanctuary to find your oak. "They will be called oaks of righteousness, a planting of the Lord for the display of his splendor" (Isa. 61:3b).

> Dear older woman, you are an Oak:
> I remember when you came and stood next to me during the Sunday worship service, leaving the pew you'd occupied for years. . . . Perhaps you were scared to venture across the sanctuary, but the Holy Spirit prompted, and you obeyed. You knew I was single and it hurt attending church service alone.
>
> I noticed your tears as you prayed for me. Yes, I was supposed to bow my head like yours, but I wanted to see your expression as you poured out your heart and petitions before the Lord on my behalf. . . . Some answers were "Yes" and some "No." If you were disappointed in God's "No," you didn't show it. You praised Him regardless and kept on praying.
>
> *You are an oak.*
>
> I'll never understand the courage it took to admit your mistakes. I'm sure you wrestled with the desire to be perfect, but know the examples of God's forgiveness in your life will stick with me forever. . . . Thank you for trying *not* to be all things to me. I have everything I need in Jesus (as you faithfully reminded me). You patiently invested in me because you rightly understood our relationship was never about you, but about you showing me Jesus.
>
> *You are an oak.*

I remember when we discussed God's calling on my life. You affirmed my spiritual gifts, helped me write my first Bible Study, and purchased one of the first copies. You pushed me out of my comfort zone, because you knew it would be for my good and, ultimately, God's glory.

I know you probably thought I was crazy leaving the corporate world for youth ministry, since women didn't attend seminary when you were my age. Yet, you realized things are different. You trusted God would open the right doors to accomplish His perfect will for me.

Over the years, you lovingly listened to my anxieties about spending the rest of my life alone. You held me as I cried through countless failed relationships. You kept me accountable for purity. You were one of the first people I called after my Air Force pilot proposed. You hand tied hundreds of white bows around chairs for my wedding reception and watched me say my wedding vows before God in His perfect timing. You believed my Chad would come. I know you were sad when I moved away to be with him. But when you call now, over four years later, I still hear your love for me.

You are an oak.

Thank you for walking through my mother's final weeks with me. My mother was grateful for you. She knew God placed you in my life to help me go forward without her. . . . I appreciate you letting me process and grieve as I watched my mother suffer. We both know you'll never replace her, but I hope you know how thankful I am God placed you in my life so I'll never feel alone as a wife and mother.

You are an oak.

Older woman, I'm writing this letter to you because young women need an oak. My prayer is you'll heed Psalm 78:1–8 and Titus 2:3–5. Don't allow fear, busyness, or inferiority to stop you from letting me . . . a younger woman . . . learn from you. Nourish us simply with your presence and prayers. You aren't here to warm a pew, precious oak, but to warm our hearts towards Jesus. The future of the church needs you. All my love,

Tracy[1]

For the LORD *is good and his love endures forever;*
his faithfulness continues through all generations.
—Psalm 100:5

INTRODUCTION

Seeking advice from others is commonplace. Some today employ the service of a personal trainer to encourage better health and physical fitness. Why not a trainer of the soul from whom we can receive help in discerning the experience of God in our lives?

—Klaus Issler[1]

Now all glory to God, who is able, through his mighty power at work within us, to accomplish infinitely more than we might ask or think. Glory to him in the church and in Christ Jesus through all generations forever and ever! Amen.

—Ephesians 3:20–21 NLT

I wrote *Mentoring for All Seasons* to awaken women to the value and blessings of participating in mentoring relationships during all stages and seasons of life.

Women often don't think they know enough to mentor, or they fear rejection if they ask someone to mentor them. Others don't understand the need for mentoring. Quite simply, many women feel *inadequate* or *indifferent*. However, throughout the Bible, specifically Titus 2:3–5, God calls spiritually younger women to learn from spiritually older women, and spiritually older women to train the younger women.

It's something so easy, and we've made it too hard. God just wants us sharing our life experiences and his faithfulness with each other. That's a concept I hope to convey to all Christian women, starting with you, the woman reading this book: *You* are the woman God wants to use as either a mentor or mentee—or the ultimate goal, both.

During the various seasons of our life, we're either the mentee needing a mentor or the mentor sharing what we've learned with a mentee going through a similar season, while looking for a mentor to help us with our next season, and so the mentoring cycle flows.

When God first put the call on my heart to start the Woman to Woman Mentoring Ministry, I had no idea what *mentoring* meant or how God would turn it into my life's ministry, passion, and purpose.

My Story: "Feed My Sheep"

In April 1995, I attended the Women in Ministry Conference in Portland, Oregon. Three years earlier, I had rededicated my life to the Lord and married my godly husband Dave. We blended our family of four children. I was attending Fuller Theological Seminary to get a Master of Arts in Christian Leadership while also managing an insurance agency. I prayerfully attended the conference, hoping the Lord would reveal where he wanted to use me when I completed seminary.

The Lord did speak to me at the conference, but not in the way I expected or in a way I had ever experienced. I was enjoying a cup of after-dinner coffee, waiting for the evening's worship and teaching to begin, when I heard a voice: "Go and feed my sheep." I looked around, but no one at the table was speaking to me. I thought, *What sheep? Where? And what would I feed them if I found them?* I heard it again: "Feed my sheep." I muttered, "Okay," and spent the rest of the evening wondering what I had just agreed to do and who was talking to me.

I couldn't wait for the evening's session to end so I could go to my room and call my husband. As I excitedly told him I thought the Lord had spoken to me, my godly husband suggested we pray for the Holy Spirit to reveal the meaning of "Feed my sheep."

The next morning, the workshop instructor said she was teaching from John 21:15–17, in which Jesus tells Peter, "Feed my sheep." As I glanced at the agenda for the day, I let out a startled "Wow!" The title of the morning's topic was "Shepherding Women in Your Church." I realized the Holy Spirit was answering our prayer.

Returning home, I asked my family and small group to pray for me to find my sheep and for direction as to what to feed them when I found them. The first sheep bleat came as a message on my business voicemail from a woman who worked in sales for the insurance company where I was a manager. Emmie lived in Northern California; I lived in Southern California.

Emmie said she was in a rehab program, and one of the assignments was to find a mentor. She saw me in a company training video wearing a necklace with a cross charm, and she wanted a Christian mentor who was successful in our business. Would I mentor her?

I was flattered and flabbergasted. I didn't have a clue what "mentoring" meant. I went to the Christian bookstore and bought *Women Encouraging Women* by the late Lucibel Van Atta, where she explains mentoring and discipleship. After reading the book, I called Emmie back and told her yes, I would mentor her. Our mentoring relationship began long distance. Emmie was chronologically my age, but spiritually younger. I wondered if perhaps "Feed my sheep" might mean *mentoring women*.

My little flock expanded when my stepdaughter asked me to sub for her in leading the young adult women's Bible study that she led in our home. I told her I would, but she should call the group members and let them know I would be leading. Everyone attended, and to my surprise, the group asked if I would continue meeting with them as a mentor. This was my first window into the younger generation's hunger for input from, and interaction with, the *older* generation. So after praying, I gladly accepted their invitation.

Several weeks later, one of the girls brought a guest. When Kristen introduced herself to the group, she said she was home for summer break from a Christian college, and her summer assignment was to find a mentor. At the end of the evening, Kristen asked if I would mentor her! I sensed Kristen was another "sheep" God wanted me to "feed," so I agreed to mentor her over the summer. My experience mentoring Kristen helped launch the Woman to Woman Mentoring Ministry at Saddleback Church.

Kristen was at a crossroads in her Christian life, trying to balance a boyfriend, school, ministry, work, friends, and family. She wanted to feel safe and secure in working through issues with a woman who would give her a godly perspective without having a personal stake in the outcome. We decided what my role in her life would be:

- A guide to and through the Scriptures
- A listening ear
- A prayer partner
- An accountability partner
- Most importantly, a role model of the Christian woman she wanted to become

Kristen asked me to mentor her because she recognized we had many things in common, and I had a life she admired and desired to achieve. She wanted to go into ministry; I was in ministry. She wanted a Christian marriage and to be a godly wife and mother; I was living out those roles. She wanted to further her Christian education; I was in seminary. She saw I had some "been there, done that" life experiences and could use what God had taught me in those situations to guide and advise her.

Kristen had loving parents, but sometimes it was difficult discussing her spiritual questions and life challenges with them. While I provided a motherly perspective, I was her spiritual mom, *not* her mom. Establishing this boundary allowed me to remain objective, and Kristen was receptive to my advice and suggestions.

When Kristen asked me to mentor her, one of my first questions was whether her mother was supportive of her having a mentor. Kristen agreed to talk with her mother and even arranged for us to meet. We had mom's blessing, but we didn't have her boyfriend's blessing. He was uncomfortable with things Kristen and I talked about because often our topic was regarding her desire to stay sexually pure under great temptation.

I also was sensitive to my own daughters' feelings about extending attention and time to another young woman. To alleviate their concerns, I had my family meet Kristen and planned a few activities for everyone to do together. I made sure my time with Kristen didn't interfere with our family's plans and activities, and I didn't talk about Kristen's issues with my family. What transpired between Kristen and me remained private.

When I first met Kristen, I was just learning about mentoring from what I read in books. But I was willing to share with her whatever insight, wisdom, and knowledge I had gleaned from life experiences and from surrendering fully to the Lord when I rededicated my life to serving him. Kristen was bold and courageous asking me to mentor her. She set herself up for possible rejection if I said no, but she determined it was worth the risk.

Kristen was honest about her struggles to stay pure and the issues she encountered at home, school, and in relationships. She asked me to keep her accountable, and I agreed. I didn't always agree with her choices and decisions, but I was there to pray with her, lead her to the Bible for answers, and make time in my schedule to meet.

I felt like a proud member of the family as I attended her wedding and got together with her periodically as her little family began to grow. Recently, I received an email with the subject line "Your First Mentee."

Woman to Woman Mentoring Ministry Birthed
Several months after accepting the call to "Feed my sheep" and starting to mentor Emmie and Kristen, the Lord divinely placed me and the young adults' pastor from Saddleback Church at the gym on the same day, at the same time. I worked out at the gym almost daily, but

this was the *only* time I *ever* saw Pastor Brad there. As he asked about my four young adult children, he mentioned that many women in his young adults group were asking where they could find a mentor.

As if God were sitting on my shoulder, I suddenly poured out my "Feed my sheep" conference story. Pastor Brad said he thought I should start a mentoring ministry at Saddleback Church, not just mentor two mentees! What? I didn't feel equipped to start a mentoring ministry at my church. After all, I had to read a book to mentor Emmie and Kristen. I did finally agree to meet with Pastor Doug, the pastor to new ministries at Saddleback at the time.

When I attended the conference in Oregon, I had specifically told the Lord I would work anywhere, *except* with women. I didn't like the way women treated each other in the business world. I was a single, career, divorced mom for seventeen years before marrying my husband Dave, and I'd never felt welcome at women's ministry events. Since I was in management and had an MBA, surely God would use me best in the business world. But was he confirming that the sheep were women and feeding was spiritual mentoring? I still didn't know how (or where) to do what I was being called to do, but I had said "Okay" to the Lord, and I would be obedient.

When I met with Pastor Doug, he agreed with Pastor Brad and handed me a guide titled "A Twelve-Step Planning Guide to Developing a Ministry at Saddleback." With both pastors' encouragement, I began going through the process of starting the Woman to Woman Mentoring Ministry at Saddleback Church and had our first Orientation Coffee at my house in January 1996.

The Lord has continued to bless this ministry. Today, God has taken the Woman to Woman Mentoring Ministry into churches around the world through a DVD leader's kit I wrote, *Woman to Woman Mentoring: How to Start, Grow, and Maintain a Mentoring Ministry*. I continue to have the opportunity to share the Woman to Woman Mentoring Ministry with churches through my speaking and writing ministry, *About His Work* Ministries. I had no idea "Feed my sheep" would go beyond Saddleback Church—even to international sheep.

Woman to Woman Mentoring is the Lord's ministry following his mandate in Titus 2:1–8: one generation of Christian men and women must teach and train the next generations. When I stepped out of my comfort zone and let God guide me in mentoring and starting a ministry, he allowed me to participate in something much bigger than I ever imagined. When I went where he called—not where I thought I should go—he molded me and made me into the mentor, ministry leader, author, speaker, wife, mother, and Grammie he wanted me to be. Along the way, he changed my heart and gave me a passion for the issues women deal with and wisdom in helping them turn to the Lord, and to each other, to navigate life's seasons. He gave me a heart for women.

I was the least likely candidate to start a women's ministry, since I had never been to a women's retreat, Bible study, small group, or special event. But I did have a willing, obedient spirit and said "Okay" to the Lord's call. I'm praying that wherever God leads you—feeding or being fed—you'll follow his call on your life too.

Mentoring for All Seasons—For Both Mentors and Mentees (M&M's)

I didn't know about mentoring when I first started Woman to Woman Mentoring, because I wasn't mentored through the challenges and crises in my own life, some of which I'll share with you in *Mentoring for All Seasons*. Where were the mentors to provide me with godly wisdom during crucial decision-making life seasons: marrying an unbeliever, divorcing, backsliding, dating, working, single parenting, remarrying, blending a family, starting a ministry?

You may be saying the same thing: *Where are the women who will mentor me?* The truth is, they're probably all around you, just like they were around me if I had made an effort to look for them.

Sometimes, we need to take the initiative. Maybe women are looking at you, wondering if you would mentor them.

Over the years, as I've taught and trained on mentoring, publishers, editors, M&M's, readers, and audiences have encouraged me to write a book on mentoring—a book to help mentors *and* mentees understand the concepts and precepts of spiritual mentoring, with practical how to's that reinforce the life-altering value of spiritual-maturity as an integral part of *all* the diversity of seasons in a Christian woman's life, from tween to twilight. *Mentoring for All Seasons: Sharing Life Experiences and God's Faithfulness* is that book.

Mentoring for All Seasons encourages women to *intentionally* share their life experiences and God's faithfulness with other women. Mentors and mentees—"M&M's"—will share stories of how mentoring blessed them in a variety of life seasons. Some of the M&M's are authors and speakers you might recognize who also share their personal mentoring experiences with you. *All* the M&M's want to encourage you to participate in mentoring relationships. These mentoring testimonies, along with my own personal experiences, helpful tips, suggestions, Scriptures, and M&M's biblical examples, will guide women in how to connect and nurture each other through mentoring relationships, as a mentor *or* a mentee. And someday, the mentee becomes a mentor.

We don't always mentor in our current season: God may put in your path a woman in a season you haven't encountered. You can look in the Table of Contents to locate the season she's in and go to that section in the book to find help in mentoring her. Mentees come from all walks and seasons of life, and even if a mentor doesn't share the exact life experience of her mentee, she can provide spiritual guidance, do research, and pray about how to address the specific issues her mentee is encountering.

Mentoring for all Seasons is a reference, application, and coaching tool for M&M's as they traverse life's journey together. I pray for Holy

Spirit inspiration for some women to become mentors. I pray for courage for others to take a step of faith and become a mentee. I pray for all to enjoy the experience of trusting God and watching how he honors your obedience to becoming Titus 2 women.

PROLOGUE

Throughout our lifetime, we vacillate between being a mentor and needing a mentor, depending on the season of life. The story of Shirley, Janine, and Kim exemplifies the blessings awaiting those who participate in God's plan for one generation mentoring the next. When they first met, Shirley was age fifty-eight and her mentees were both thirty-four. When they shared this story, Shirley was seventy-six, Janine and Kim were fifty-four, and the mentoring continues through their Friends of the Heart ministry.

Mentor *Shirley Brosius* Shares

We've studied with our heads together, cried on each other's shoulders, and laughed so hard we couldn't talk. In 1998, two women in my congregation—women young enough to be my daughters—asked me to mentor them. I had previously served on a church staff, Kim was just starting out in a staff position, and Janine was an active volunteer. I wasn't sure what these women expected, but I agreed because Titus 2:3–5 encourages mentoring.

Sitting on the floor of my home office so as not to disturb my sleeping husband, the three of us began meeting once a week at 5:30 A.M.—Kim and Janine wanted to meet before their husbands left for work to eliminate the need for babysitting. Now that their children are young adults, we meet at 4 P.M.

Since each of us was already involved in a Bible study group, we chose to read and discuss Christian books. Mentoring has offered many blessings. We have grown closer to God and to each other as our HEARTS have knit together:

- **H**ope: Kim and Janine say I give them hope because, by God's grace, I've survived many of life's storms—deaths, childrearing, and ministry challenges, to name a few—with my faith intact. They ask questions; I give honest answers.
- **E**ncouragement: I see things from a different generation's perspective, so I encourage them to view the bigger picture.
- **A**ccountability: We take turns leading our sessions and close with a challenge. The next week we compare notes on how we handled the challenge.
- **R**efuge: Through the years, our trust has grown. Without shame, we confess our failures and weaknesses and accept one another as we are.
- **T**eaching: Each of us excels in some area and teaches the others. Kim speaks in her professional life and as a leader in her church. Janine easily establishes relationships. And I offer a model of love for the Word of God since I memorize extensive portions of Scripture.
- **S**ervice: Our study time challenged us to serve God together. We developed a women's retreat and offered it to churches. Now we speak at women's retreats and

other events about twenty times a year as "Friends of the Heart." We also coauthored a women's devotional, *Turning Guilt Trips into Joy Rides*.

Outside of my family, my mentoring relationship with Kim and Janine is the most blessed relationship in my life. Just search out someone older or younger you want to get to know better and do what comes naturally—that's mentoring.

Mentee *Kim Messinger* Shares

People ask about my mentoring journey with Shirley and Janine. To be honest, I'm not a detailed, note-taking person. Had I known on the cold, dark morning of January 5, 1998, that the start to something extraordinary was happening, even I would have scribbled a few lines on a napkin.

I'm sure our first meeting for prayer and sharing was no different than any other first meeting—except we're still meeting eighteen years later! Over the years, I've told the story with tear-filled eyes to countless women of how our meetings, woven through nearly two decades, have made me the woman I am today. I love when the three of us are together! I love even more when we serve together as Friends of the Heart.

One of the greatest blessings is when we prepare for a Friends of the Heart event, which usually begins with a discussion around Shirley's kitchen table. One year we asked, "Who would be blessed by a friendship tea?" In different seasons: "Let's do a prayer event! People can email or Facebook us prayer requests!" Then, "Let's visit a nursing home." We each have roles and responsibilities. Shirley is the event planner, Janine the "Keeper of the Books," and I cover sound details.

Friends of the Heart ministry started from two young gals asking a more mature, very together, woman to walk beside them as a mentor. Without each other, we wouldn't have experienced the joy of speaking for Jesus as a team, or meeting and ministering to so many women. #mentoringworks!

Mentee *Janine Boyer* Shares

Mentoring was something I believed every Christian should experience in his or her walk with the Lord. A "Paul" mentor who has been a Christian longer trains and encourages a "Timothy" mentee who is younger in the faith. I believe the Lord was challenging me (and Kim) to be a Timothy and ask Shirley to be our Paul. But Shirley's mature faith intimidated me. Was I ready to accept the wisdom Shirley's life journey could teach me? However, since Kim and I had experienced ministering together, I realized God had already placed a godly woman and friend in my life to lean on, learn from, and lunge forward with, so together we took the plunge and asked Shirley to be our mentor. I couldn't be more grateful for these two women. I quickly learned mentoring isn't intimidating . . . it's full of love, grace, and the challenge to grow in my own personal journey with the Lord.

Shirley never professed she was the perfect Christian. Instead, she came alongside us as our friend. She listened, encouraged, and prayed for us. As we continued meeting over the years, I welcomed Shirley's and Kim's honest feedback. I didn't always hear what I wanted, but I knew I was getting the truth, rooted in God's Word. They helped me focus on God's purposes when I wanted to follow my own direction. When they asked tough questions, their skills and experiences challenged me to learn, grow, and develop. I trusted them with *every* part of my life.

Eighteen years later, I think of Jesus's message to his followers in John 15:15, "I have called you friends, for everything that I learned from my Father I have made known to you." We all need friends who help each other live for the cause of Christ. It still amazes me, and I'm forever grateful, that Shirley said yes to two young mothers trying to find their way through life. Mentors bring out the best in you . . . you just need to be willing to let them into your life.

CHRISTIAN MENTORING 101

A mentor is willing to make a relational life-to-life investment and walk with you through her life journey and yours.
—Pat Ennis

One generation commends your works to another; they tell of your mighty acts.
—Psalm 145:4

CHAPTER ONE

MENTORING IS NOT OPTIONAL

Through supernatural provision in each major season of my life, God placed just the right women who would mentor and help me through— during my teen years, in my single adult/dating years, and as a young wife and mom. It was a process to finally soar on my own and seek him with all my heart. All the mentors God has blessed me with are still a part of my life.

—Shelly

What does it take to pour into the life of another? The mention of it overwhelms us. We think we have to have it all figured out before we dare to think we have anything to offer. All the while, there are women who hunger for the mentor/discipleship friendships that offer a safe space to grow.

—Karen Trigg[1]

You have heard me teach things that have been confirmed by many reliable witnesses. Now teach these truths to other trustworthy people who will be able to pass them on to others.

—2 Timothy 2:2 NLT

What Is a Christian Mentor?

The term *mentor* is familiar in the business world: a guide, counselor, teacher, and instructor. Mentors provide experience, knowledge, achievements, position, and, most importantly, willingness to share with someone else. They encourage mentees to aspire to the mentor role themselves someday. Emmie, from the Introduction, asked me to mentor her because I was successful in our insurance company, but Emmie also wanted a *Christian* mentor, who was

- Wise and knowledgeable in the Word of God
- A trusted confidant
- Willing to counsel, instruct, and guide her in how to live in a Christlike way

Wisdom comes from God speaking and working through the Christian mentor. God inspires her thoughts when she prays and allows God to teach her through her life experiences. She discovers that with Christ's help, we learn from our mistakes, as well as our good decisions, and we can share these life lessons with another woman going through something similar. "My mouth will speak words of wisdom; the meditation of my heart will give you understanding" (Ps. 49:3).

Trusted implies confidence to share our innermost feelings with someone and the assurance they will keep it confidential. We also trust their counsel because we know their wisdom is God inspired. "Listen, for I have trustworthy things to say; I open my lips to speak what is right" (Prov. 8:6).

A *counselor* and advisor is someone who helps us learn how to go to the one true Counselor: the Lord and his Word, the Bible. "But the Advocate, the Holy Spirit, whom the Father will send in my name, will teach you all things and will remind you of everything I have said to you" (John 14:26).

Mentor Julie experienced how easy it really is to be a Christian mentor:

> My pastor asked me to mentor a young woman at our church. I didn't really know what a mentor did, but this beautiful gal and I got together for tea once a week while my kids were at karate. We just sat and talked. I'd ask her questions about how life was going in various arenas of her world: spiritual, friends, work, and family. Sometimes, she'd ask me a question about how I handled things. I guess that's mentoring.

What Is a Mentee?

Since our discussion is about *Christian* mentoring, our answer to *What is a mentee?* will differ from the secular or business world's definition. Regardless of age, any woman in a new season of life—whether or not she's a Christian—needs a godly role model. She needs someone who will help her understand how to live as a woman, mother, wife, daughter, sister, single parent, divorcée, dating single, widow, grandmother, career woman, neighbor . . . maybe even new believer.

A woman could be a mentee at any stage, age, or season of life. Maybe she didn't experience a Christian home environment or didn't have healthy parenting or marriage role models. Perhaps she has no one to go to for Christian advice and wise counsel. Her original decision for Christ may have alienated her from family and friends. Perhaps, like me, she accepted Christ at an early age, later backslid, and then rededicated her life to Christ and now needs help staying on track with the Lord. Or she's having trouble relying on God during tragedies and chaos, or just the everyday challenges of her life.

Every woman experiences new seasons of life in which she needs someone who will help her live out her faith. Throughout life, we navigate between being a mentor and needing a mentor, because life is never static. We come out of one season, only to go straight into the next unknown season. We should always have a mentor and be a mentor: "Follow my example, as I follow the example of Christ" (1 Cor. 11:1). You can do that . . . right?

What Is Intentional Mentoring?

You may have heard the buzzword "organic mentoring." Proponents champion the idea of mentoring happening naturally, as women encounter each other in daily life. They tout that spiritually older women will *organically* seek out spiritually younger women and vice versa. But I'm sure you would agree that in our fast-paced lives, even if we know we *should* mentor, how many actually *do* take a spiritually younger woman under our wing? Or how many women are brave enough to ask another woman to mentor them? I'm thrilled to share stories in Section Two from M&M's who have enjoyed the blessings of Titus 2 mentoring relationships. Tragically, for every one of these uplifting true stories, thousands of women are alone and struggling through a season of life—depressed, discouraged, distraught, discontent, and disengaged from the church and the Lord.

If Christian women were organically mentoring other women on a regular basis, I guarantee the number of women experiencing divorces, drug overuse, alcoholism, eating disorders, addictions, depression, illnesses, and suicides would decrease . . . maybe even diminish all together. The multitudes of women struggling in daily life and floundering in their faith are evidence that *organic* mentoring isn't working. Women need *intentional* mentoring.

Every Christian is in a continual process of learning and growing in the knowledge of Christ until we meet him face-to-face. But until that day, we who are further along in our walk with the Lord, or have navigated through a life season, must be willing to *intentionally* share with another woman what we *do* know and what the Lord *has done* in our lives.

Often people ask, "Wouldn't it be better to call the Woman to Woman Mentoring Ministry a friendship or discipleship ministry?" God spoke clearly to me. He wanted "feeding," or mentoring, to

- Be more than a typical friendship
- Include discipling when appropriate
- Always focus on spiritual maturity
- Address the numerous mentoring needs during the multitude of seasons in a woman's life

For example, a woman may have been a Christian since childhood, but now she's in a season of life she's never been in before (perhaps as a college student, military wife, career woman, or mother), so she doesn't need discipleship; she needs a Christian mentor who has lived through this experience and can help her navigate her new life season. A friendship might also be formed, but mentoring goes beyond a friendship. M&M's are two women—mentor and mentee—looking at God's plan for their lives in a specific season. Klaus Issler offers a good summation of spiritual mentoring:

> Spiritual mentoring is different from pastoral counseling or psychological therapy in which problem solving, decision making and "fixing" the person are the major concerns. Furthermore, it is not purely a theological discussion of Christian doctrine or the nature of God. Rather, it is a dialogue about our relationship with God as evident in the experiences of our life. The mentor helps us learn how to discern God's movement within our life experiences. To what extent in this experience are we moving toward God or away from him? Where is God in this experience? What might God be saying in this experience? Or are we mostly self-absorbed about the matter? Mentoring involves a voluntary relationship of confidentiality and accountability, rather than one of authority over another.[2]

What Does Scripture Instruct about Mentoring?

There are numerous verses in both the Old and New Testament where God clearly says we are to mentor each other: One generation should teach and train the next generation. We will look at many in this book, but here are just a few Old Testament verses: Deut. 4:9, 6:6–9; Ps. 71:18, 78:4, 79:13, 145:4–7; Joel 1:2–3.

The most familiar verses cited for mentoring are Titus 2:1–8 from the New Testament, where Paul tells Titus, the young pastor of a new church in Crete, what the role is for spiritually older men and women.

I like *The Message* translation. Notice what Paul says is the "job" of every Christian:

> *Your job is to speak out on the things that make for solid doctrine.* Guide older men into lives of temperance, dignity, and wisdom, into healthy faith, love, and endurance. Guide older women into lives of reverence so they end up as neither gossips nor drunks, but models of goodness. By looking at them, the younger women will know how to love their husbands and children, be virtuous and pure, keep a good house, be good wives. We don't want anyone looking down on God's Message because of their behavior. Also, guide the young men to live disciplined lives.
>
> *But mostly, show them all this by doing it yourself, incorruptible in your teaching, your words solid and sane.* Then anyone who is dead set against us, when he finds nothing weird or misguided, might eventually come around. (Titus 2:1–8 *The Message*—emphasis added)

Each generation has a predisposition to look at God as the God of the past who doesn't understand the current culture with its issues. That's why I'm such a passionate proponent of mentoring and living out Titus 2:1–8, where spiritually older men and women receive the charge to teach, train, and model the Christian life to *all* generations so they won't be deceived and dissuaded from their faith. To understand the full impact of Titus 2:1–8, we need to read the issues Paul was addressing in the previous verses. It sounds a lot like our world today:

> Everything is pure to those whose hearts are pure. But nothing is pure to those who are corrupt and unbelieving, because their minds and consciences are corrupted. Such people claim they know God, but they deny him by the way they live. They are detestable and disobedient, worthless for doing anything good. (Titus 1:15–16 NLT)

Titus 2:1–8 was Paul's antidote for guiding the next generation of believers to discern between corrupt, detestable, disobedient mistruths of deceivers and the true teachings of obedient followers of Jesus Christ and his Word, the Bible.

Mentors aren't always *chronologically* older, but they are always *spiritually* older. Maybe not by very much, but they should have a little more experience walking with the Lord than their mentee. God will always put someone in your path needing to hear how he worked in and through your life experiences and that he'll be there in the same way for her too. The verses in Titus are enhanced by 1 Thessalonians 2:7–8, 12, which emphasizes the nurturing, encouraging characteristic of mentoring:

> Just as a nursing mother cares for her children, so we cared for you. Because we loved you so much, we were delighted to share with you not only the gospel of God but our lives as well. . . . encouraging, comforting and urging you to live lives worthy of God, who calls you into his kingdom and glory.

Paul closes out Titus 2 with this admonition, which could apply to mentors: "You must teach these things *and encourage the believers to do them*. You have the authority to correct them when necessary, so don't let anyone disregard what you say" (Titus 2:15 NLT—emphasis added).

Sixty-eight-year-old Paulette, a mother of five and grandmother of eight, and married for forty-nine years, explains why she mentors in obedience to Titus 2:

> My initial motivation to be a mentor in our church mentoring ministry was a concern for today's young women. If the church doesn't teach them, the world will—"reality" TV offers *unreal* role models like a soft-spoken, stay-at-home mom who homeschools her many well-behaved

children and smiles adoringly at her loving husband, or the *unreal* "Real Housewives" who are outwardly beautiful but inwardly immature, petty, self-absorbed, ungrateful, and often immoral. Where are the real-life Christian role models?

I saw the mentoring ministry as an opportunity for the church to show women a better way, God's way. Titus 2:3–5 calls the older women to teach the younger women. What I hadn't considered, and have now learned, is each woman— regardless of age—needs at least one other woman to listen to her, pray for her, encourage her, and, when needed, speak truth to her. I encourage the mentees after their mentoring relationships to come alongside a woman the Lord puts in their paths and be there for her as their mentors were there for them.

Many churches call asking for advice on how to encourage the women of their churches to become involved in mentoring. To all, I reply, "Take your women to Titus 2:1–8, where the Lord scripturally *commands all* Christian men and women to teach the spiritually younger men and women."

Next, I suggest there are *no qualifiers* in this passage. These verses don't say "Older women, teach the younger women *if* you have time, feel like it, can fit it into your schedule, aren't doing another ministry, don't work, or feel comfortable or qualified doing it." They simply say to just do it! This passage is the job description for women who know Christ: "Your job is to speak out on the things that make for solid doctrine" (Titus 2:1 *The Message*).

WHY WE NEED MENTORING

Life is complicated. When we're going through difficult days, we need a true friend we can turn to for help. A mentor can be the friend who puts her arms around us, comfort us, listens, and prays for us in the good and bad days.

—Rosalie

Where there is no guidance the people fall,
But in abundance of counselors there is victory.

—Proverbs 11:14 NASB

Let the wise listen and add to their learning,
and let the discerning get guidance.

—Proverbs 1:5

Every generation longs for and needs other Christ followers to learn from and experience not only the greatness of God's love and mercy, but also how to live it out in daily life. In Titus 2:5, 8, Paul emphasizes why spiritually older women and men are to teach the spiritually younger: "We don't want anyone looking down on God's Message *because of their behavior*" (Titus 2:5 *The Message*), "so that no one *will malign the word of God*" (2:5), or "have nothing bad to say about us" (2:8—emphasis added).

But we *do* see the Word of God maligned and looked down on today, and Christians are often denounced and discriminated against. Paul emphasized that Christians should reflect Christ in actions, relationships, marriages, and interactions with the culture: a living witness and mentoring testimony to encourage others to come to know Christ, not turn away. Our Christian lives should further, not hinder, the spread of the gospel. *Knowing* what to do must transform into *living* what you know.

Christians believe the Bible is the inerrant, inspired Word of God, and the entire Bible applies to *every* Christian. We can't choose verses that are easy to follow and discard those we don't like or find challenging. Yet many disregard biblical directives from God, like Titus 2:1–8, as applicable for the church in Crete two thousand years ago, because they can't possibly apply to churches in today's culture. That's a big mistake. The Bible is timeless and as relevant today as it was in Paul and Titus' day: "Jesus Christ is the same yesterday and today and forever" (Heb. 13:8).

There are few commands in the Bible this gender specific. The Lord seldom says specifically, *Women, you do this for me.* However, in Titus 2:3–5, he did!

Many young women in the church, and in today's culture, are struggling in their roles as wives, mothers, friends, employees, singles, or new believers, and sometimes just in being a woman. Where are the spiritually older women who will selflessly reach out to the spiritually younger women or the women in new seasons of life?

How many of you relate to the sad testimony I've heard from many women who said they walked out of a crusade, revival meeting, or church service where they accepted Christ as their Lord and Savior, and then went right back into their old lifestyle? One woman said she even went to a party with her worldly friends the very night she accepted Christ! Why do so many women backslide and go years with Christ in their head but not in their heart? Their stories all say something similar:

> I know I accepted Christ. I asked him into my heart but
> didn't know what it meant. My old familiar life and friends
> and unsaved family were all still there, but no one from
> this "new life" offered to help me learn how to live it. It just

seemed easier to go on as I had before. Only now, I had a
lot of confusion, guilt, and conviction, which made me feel
even worse than before accepting Jesus as my Savior.

Haven't you heard these stories yourself? Maybe it's *your* story. We
would never think of sending our babies out on their own as soon as
they could walk and talk. Yet we send baby Christians out the doors
of our churches into the secular world without a hand to hold to keep
them safe until they become spiritually mature. With such a wealth
of wisdom in the women of our churches, who have so much to offer
simply from living life with Christ, this is tragic. They have the knowledge and experience to help these spiritually younger Christians find
the answers to their life and faith questions.

Taking the time to reach out to a spiritually younger woman is
a selfless act of giving and ministry: letting your life—with all the
wealth of good and bad experiences—testify to how Christ was with
you through it all. There are women in your church desperately in
need of a mentor who will honor the commands given to each of us
in Titus 2 to teach them how to study and apply God's Word to their
lives. Show them how to be godly, moral, righteous Christian women
in an ungodly, immoral, unrighteous world. Who is assuming responsibility to transmit biblical values to these women in your church?
Who is listening to their questions and concerns and guiding them
to the one book with all the answers—the Bible—and the One who
fulfills all their needs?

I commend those of you who have accepted God's call to mentor.
I know you received an incredible blessing in return. God gave us
the Titus 2 command as a blessing, not a burden. When we make an
investment in a spiritually younger woman, it enriches our own lives,
the sense of connectedness and shepherding in our church families
deepens, society benefits, and we honor God's Word.

Jesus said, "Truly I tell you, anyone who gives you a cup of water in my name because you belong to the Messiah will certainly not lose their reward" (Mark 9:41). You can't out-give God. As we share our life with another sister in Christ, our own life and our church will receive immeasurable blessings.

Section Two has inspiring stories from M&M's in various seasons of life. If you've experienced a mentoring relationship and the life-changing blessings, share your testimony with other women who may have questions or are hesitant to mentor or be a mentee. Read Titus 2:3–5 again and pray about making these verses a permanent and ongoing part of your Christian walk as a mentor. If you were a mentee, someone is right where you were just a short time ago, and she could use your encouragement and mentoring. "What you heard from me, keep as the pattern of sound teaching, with faith and love in Christ Jesus. Guard the good deposit that was entrusted to you—guard it with the help of the Holy Spirit who lives in us" (2 Tim. 1:13–14).

If you're a spiritually younger woman seeking a mentor, don't give up looking for her. Read on and I'll help you find her. Tina Wilson[1] overcame her fear of finding mentors and you can too!

The thought of finding a mentor left me feeling like I was in middle school again without a date to the dance. How would I find someone to help in all areas of my life? Maybe I would ask someone already close. Only everyone around me was at the same place in life I was.

Outside my circles, I was incredibly fearful of asking someone to mentor me because the thought of rejection was crippling. The people I would love to ask were so busy already; why would they make time for me? Those horrible "what if's" stopped me. Surely, someone would notice the hungry-for-more look on my face.

Just as I was ready to move on and do the best I could with what information I had, I heard a message about mentoring that opened my eyes to exponential possibilities. It said, "To assume *one* person could mentor you in *all* areas of your life is saying she's next to Jesus in perfection . . . no *one* person could possibly speak into *every area*. Look for people who are at the place you want to be in *each* area of life and ask them questions about that one place."

So I did. I got in a room with women stronger than me in a few areas of life and just listened to them talk. It awakened my spirit to possibilities and allowed me to see new things and experience one aha moment after another. These ladies had strong marriages, and the more I listened, they were actually speaking highly of their spouses! It set a standard of respect never modeled to me before.

The more I learned, the more I craved. I noticed changes in my attitude—the way I viewed my marriage, kids, career, and choices. Every time I felt a need to change, I leaned into the Lord and His Word. My relationship grew stronger with Him, and now I understand the Lord is the root from which everything grows. He constantly leads people in and out of my life to teach, speak into, and mentor me. I have a few ladies who model

- True submission in their marriage, without feeling railroaded
- Christlike business practices, helping me understand why I don't always have to win or come out on top
- Parenting that sometimes means denying my desires
- Being the Lord's servant, because sacrificially giving time and resources I've *earned* isn't my natural response
- Discipline in eating and exercise habits not ingrained in me

Nothing replaces a great example. I need someone to
show me how to walk out the Christian life . . . even better,
someone willing *to walk with me* until I figure it out. The
people who I allow to influence my life walk their talk;
their actions speak louder than their words.

CHAPTER THREE

GENERATION GAPS
ARE NOT IN GOD'S PLAN

We as women have a responsibility to impact the generations behind us to live out God's purpose in our lives. I have had amazing women who have helped me realize that, and I am purposely trying to pass that down to my own daughter and nieces on a daily basis. While I am far from perfect, I have a Savior who is flawless, and being real, transparent and seeking God's guidance are all important parts of mentorship.

—Missy Robertson[1]

Whether one calls it "mentor" or "friend," engaging with another in cross-generational conversation will deepen your understanding of what is most important in life—faith, family, and friends. The generation gap melts away as we gain honor for what each person has to offer. So, these days, I always like to have a younger woman I'm personally investing in and an older woman to whom I look to pour life into me. Those relationships almost always form with unexpected people.

—Tahni Cullen

Let each generation tell its children of your mighty acts;
let them proclaim your power.

—Psalm 145:4 NLT

Why Do We Have Generation Gaps?

It was never God's plan to have generation gaps in the church: God commanded one generation to pass down his truths to the next generation. But in most churches today, the gap between generations is so wide that the only thing passed between the two is mistrust and misunderstanding—all in the name of Jesus.

I believe the older generation often perpetuates the gap by wanting everything to stay the same—*same* music, *same* way of doing things, *same* church service, *same* church activities. . . . Many churches relegate the young people to their own groups, and their input—whether in music or new ideas or using their talents and gifts—isn't welcome in the main sanctuary. Then the church wonders why the youth and young adults are leaving in droves.

Church isn't about us. The purpose of worship isn't solely to focus *inward*, but *outward*. We don't attend church simply for spiritual feeding—although that's an important aspect. We're to take what we learn and *pass it on to others*. The great commission compels us to tell the world about Jesus—*especially* the next generation.

> Then Jesus came to them and said, "All authority in heaven
> and on earth has been given to me. Therefore go and make
> disciples of all nations, baptizing them in the name of the
> Father and of the Son and of the Holy Spirit, and teaching
> them to obey everything I have commanded you. And
> surely I am with you always, to the very end of the age."
> (Matt. 28:18–20)

If we want to stay relevant in the lives of the next generation, we need to learn how to embrace *their* style of worship . . . *their* way of communicating . . . *their* world. If we want to have an impact in *their* lives—to help guide them in the ways of righteousness—we need to speak *their* language, care about the things *they* care about, and reach out to them in love with a desire to understand what's important to *them*.

It's vital that the older generation keep up with current communication technology—or let the younger generation teach us how to use it. Texting is the main means of communication today with the younger generation, and as each of our grandchildren receives a cell phone, we make sure they have our cell number programmed into their phone. When I don't understand something about my cell phone, I ask my grandson. The younger generation loves to show the older generation how to adapt to their world. They don't expect us to know all the latest trends, but they do expect us to show an interest in learning about them.

When I rededicated my life to the Lord in the summer of 1992, it marked a turning point. I moved from thinking of how I could further *myself in this world* to how I could further *God's earthly kingdom*. When I asked what God was calling me to do, he clearly answered. I was to take a huge risk of leaving a well-paying career to go into full-time lay ministry. Not just any ministry—a mentoring ministry to engage women of all ages, seasons of life, and stages of faith to grow and mature spiritually together. That was twenty years ago, and God continues to take Woman to Woman Mentoring into churches around the world.

You don't have to start a ministry, but what is God asking you to do to help close the generation gap?

What Is Your Generation Doing?

There is a question each generation must ask and answer: What does God call believers—you and me—to do today? Each of us must answer in a personal and introspective way. How can we invest our lives in the next generation—the future?

- Mothers, invest in your children.
- Grandmothers, invest in your grandchildren.
- Employers, invest in your employees.
- Ministry leaders, invest in your team members.
- Pastors, invest in your congregation.
- Neighbors, invest in your community.
- School teachers and Sunday school teachers, invest in your students.
- Leaders, invest in your followers.

- Youth leaders, invest in the future of the church.
- Mentors, invest in your mentees.
- Mentees, after you're mentored, become a mentor and invest in a mentee.

Mentoring: A Privilege, Not a Burden

Do you remember when you were the next generation, full of hope and ideas and ready to leave your mark on the world? I do. I also remember feeling misunderstood and unappreciated when sharing thoughts and ideas with older adults. Yet thirty-six times in the New Living Translation of the Bible, the Lord uses the term "generation to generation." Many more verses instruct us to pour into those who are coming up behind us in the church and in our homes. It was God's plan for the continuation of his church throughout the generations.

Believers are to teach and train the next generation. Praise God, over the centuries believers have followed this mandate. You and I are benefactors of the sacrifices of believers who have gone before us. Over the years, followers of God and his Son, Jesus Christ, have felt compelled to ensure the next generation

- Has access to and knowledge of the Bible
- Knows how to communicate with God through the Holy Spirit and prayer
- Receives guidance in leading a godly life

Sharing with the next generation some of what God and life have taught us is truly an honor and a privilege. "I will bring honor to your name in every generation. Therefore, the nations will praise you forever and ever" (Ps. 45:17 NLT).

The blessings multiply when the next generation is teachable and eager to learn, as Esther discovered:

When we retired, I offered a summer Bible study in my home. Mary, a young newlywed, signed up first. The Lord prompted me to ask if she would like me to mentor her. Mary said she never would've asked me, because once she asked someone who was too busy. Now, I intentionally ask whomever the Lord leads me to if she would like a mentor; everyone says yes. I love seeing who he'll bring next. I count it a *privilege to mentor*.

A Plea from the Younger Generation

I often hear from the older generation that the reason they don't mentor is because the younger generation isn't interested in being mentored, but this is a misconception and lie of the enemy. Tracey is a young twenty-something wife and mother, passionate about her growing relationship with Christ, and like so many young women, desperate for a mentor. I pray older women take Tracey's plea to heart, because *every* church has a Tracey and her friends.

Nothing is more confusing than being a young woman living in today's society. This world and the media offer twisted views of women. A lack of discipleship causes many young women, including myself, to stray from the truth or to have a misconception of its value. As a young and relatively new Christian, I've had numerous conversations with friends about the desire for a more authentic relationship with the Lord. However, all agree we don't know what that looks like because we aren't around it enough. We haven't received wisdom, discernment, and accountability to become the kind of women the Lord wants us to be . . . and we want to become.

Today, most women my age find identity through success in work, their bodies, and attention from men. We no longer look for respect, because we stopped receiving it long ago, or never experienced it.

I plead for so many others, and myself, who have no idea what it looks like to be a godly woman. If I could share one truth with an older woman interested in investing in a lost generation, it would be this: we *need* your commitment and honesty. Don't feel inferior or believe in the "age gap." Every woman 15 to 105 faces temptations, battles, and triumphs. We need advice on everything! Since older women have experienced much more in life, younger women look to them as examples.

I *beg* the older generations to please be the mentors God called you to be—take up your cross and invest in the future. It takes patience, perseverance, and Christianity. The women you invest in today may turn around and invest in tomorrow's generation. "Then Jesus said to his disciples, 'Whoever wants to be my disciple must deny themselves and take up their cross and follow me'" (Matthew 16:24).[2]

WHO CAN MENTOR, AND WHO WILL MENTOR ME?

CHAPTER FOUR

Our evangelical women's ministry is ignoring the Titus 2:3–5 mentoring model. Have the younger women become less teachable or have the older women failed to teach?

—Pat Ennis

As iron sharpens iron,
so one person sharpens another.

—Proverbs 27:17

My tagline for mentoring is the subtitle for this book: *Sharing Life Experiences and God's Faithfulness.* Have you seen God at work in your life? Then share your story with another woman who may be going through something similar or needs encouragement in a particular season of life and her walk with the Lord. Then help her discover answers to her questions and life issues, through prayer and the Bible. Mentoring is always a two-way relationship. As you search the Bible together, pray for God's guidance and wisdom, and wait for answers. Proverbs 3:5–7 (NLT) clearly tells us,

> Trust in the LORD with all your heart;
> do not depend on your own understanding.
> Seek his will in all you do,
> and he will show you which path to take.
> Don't be impressed with your own wisdom.
> Instead, fear the LORD and turn away from evil.

From this passage, we can conclude three things about mentoring:

1. *Trust* and have confidence in God to reveal his will. Don't place the weight of a decision, answer, or suggestion on your own understanding or intelligence and insight.
2. *Seek* his will, which doesn't change according to your circumstances or desires.
3. *Acknowledge* God's authority by turning to his Word.

Our areas of expertise can be our greatest hindrance to our faith if we trust more in *our* knowledge than the *supernatural*. In Section Two, each life experience season has a section titled God's Perspective: Search the Scriptures Together, with suggested Scripture passages for the M&M's to study and discuss together to arrive at God's will and perspective on issues related to that season. The Appendix also has suggestions for how to look up more verses on specific topics.

Jesus was the *only* perfect mentor. Pride and a sense of false humility keep many women from mentoring. No one expects you to have the Bible memorized or be a Bible scholar to qualify as a mentor; you just need to have lived life, observed God at work in the seasons of your life, and seek the guidance of the Holy Spirit. There are plenty of resources available today to help you look up a Bible verse or research a topic. As my daughter says, "Mom, you can find everything by googling." Just remember, Scripture is the foundation for all mentoring: "All Scripture is God-breathed and is useful for teaching, rebuking, correcting and training in righteousness, so that the servant of God may be thoroughly equipped for every good work" (2 Tim. 3:16–17).

As a mentee learns to depend on God and his Word in her life seasons, through the guidance, prayers, and support of her mentor, she can then help another woman going through similar seasons. Thus, the cycle of life and mentoring carries down through the generations—God's plan for the propagation of Christianity and the church.

Mentoring occurs in all seasons of life—in the good and the challenging times. One woman shares with another her "been there, done that" life experiences and how with God's help she made it through, and the mentee will too. God never wastes a hurt. He simply asks us to use *all* our experiences to mentor someone else. You will continue meeting women with similar circumstances as yours, and the Holy Spirit will tug at your heart to reach out to her. If you miss the opportunity, there will be another one, and another one . . . you can be sure.

A message from Anna asking me to mentor her reveals what so many women feel today: an urgent call for women to understand we must be mentoring in all seasons.

> At forty-five, there are few mentors. In my twenties and thirties, it was easy to find an older mentor. Perhaps in my forties, *I'm* expected to mentor . . . although, I don't feel prepared. I know there are many women in my church I could go to; however, I'm closer to those my age and younger. When you and I met on vacation, I felt God was putting you in my bank of "people he places in your life" . . . and as I struggle with issues, you keep popping into my mind, via Facebook, thoughts, and prayer.

My friend and fellow author, Crystal Bowman, challenges us to mentor the "Annas" God brings into our paths:

> I don't have any counseling degrees qualifying me to be a mentor. I just love God and want to share my life's experience and wisdom with younger women. If you have a passion for mentoring, ask God to show you what he wants you to do. And when he calls you to a mentoring opportunity, he will equip you. You'll be a blessing to the people you mentor, and they'll be a blessing to you.

MENTORING IN A WORLD FORSAKING GOD

When I was in my mid-thirties, I sat under the teaching of an older woman in my church, Mary Marshal Young. She opened my eyes to the truths in Scripture.[1] I was trying to take hold of what God had for me, but refusing to let go of what He didn't. And then I met Mary. She began to teach me about who I was as a child of God: holy, dearly loved, anointed, appointed, chosen, valuable to God, indwelt by the Holy Spirit. She showed me I was free from condemnation and enveloped in grace. Mary explained the truth of my new identity under the muck and mire of my stuck faith and encouraged me to move forward and live bold. . . . I knew the truth in my head, but had trouble believing it was true for me.

—Sharon Jaynes[2]

Obey the Word of God. If you hear only and do not act, you are only fooling yourself.

—James 1:22 NLV

We live in tumultuous times in both the church and the world. Confusion and fear reign among newer believers who don't have a solid foundation in the truth to help them discern evil from good, lies from truths, abnormal from normal. If more women would reach out to each other with understanding, prayer, and biblical truths, there would be far less fear, confusion, backsliding, and sin in women's lives.

Since Adam and Eve ate the forbidden fruit in the Garden of Eden, every generation has lived in a fallen world. What one generation did in moderation, the next generation does in excess. Just as the apostle Paul saw the need for mentors in his day, we desperately need mentors today. Yet many who should be stepping up to mentor and teach the next generation are falling away from Titus 2, just as quickly as our world is falling away from God.

What Can We Do?

So how do we ordinary Christian women make a difference in today's chaotic and fallen world? As mentors, we speak, teach, and train the truth to our mentees, straight from the Bible. So we must daily read our Bibles and let God's Word speak, teach, and train the truth to us so we can respond to life's issues from God's perspective. Together, M&M's learn spiritual wisdom and scriptural principles to help navigate the moral decline of our culture and, in some cases, the foundation of the Christian faith. God confirms this truth in Isaiah 48:17:

> This is what the Lord says—
> your Redeemer, the Holy One of Israel:
> "I am the Lord your God,
> who teaches you what is best for you,
> who directs you in the way you should go."

How Does Titus 2 Apply to Today's Culture?

I like the J.B. Phillips New Testament translation of Titus 2 for this discussion. Again, think of old and young in terms of *spiritually older* and *spiritually younger*. The apostle Paul is explaining to the young pastor Titus how mentoring works in Crete, a pagan and sinful culture, much like today.

> Now you must tell them the sort of character which
> should spring from sound teaching. The [spiritually older]
> old men should be temperate, serious, wise—spiritually
> healthy through their faith and love and patience. (Titus
> 2:1–2 PHILLIPS)

Paul tells Titus to provide sound teaching to the spiritually older men so they will be spiritually mature, wise, patient, and full of love as they lead their homes and teach the younger men (2:6–8). Then *likewise*, these same things said to the men also apply to the women, along with areas specific to women:

> Similarly, the [spiritually older] old women should be reverent in their behaviour, should not make unfounded complaints and should not be over-fond of wine. (2:3 PHILLIPS)

- Synonyms for *reverent* are worshipful, respectful, and humble. We certainly don't see these characteristics modeled much today, especially in the entertainment or media industries, which influence so many women.
- Other translations replace *unfounded complaints* with *not gossiping or slandering others*. In Paul's day, women were limited to gossiping and spreading rumors by word of mouth, but today we have telephones, texting, email, and social media, where a misspoken word about, or inappropriate picture of, someone can spread like wildfire and do just as much damage. Young women are often clueless about the harm they're doing when they taunt another girl or bully her, because it's often the norm in movies or TV, or there's no supervision of electronics at home. Or perhaps the girls actually learn how to gossip at home by overhearing Mom on the phone or seeing her social media posts. All too often, bullied young women are driven to depression, self-harm, or even suicide.
- The reference to *over-fond of wine* could apply to any substance addiction. Unfortunately, many young moms drink alcohol to excess. There are websites and Facebook

groups with titles like "Winey Moms" or "Moms Who Need Wine," with the theme that they can't make it through a day of mothering without wine. And this is considered laughable and normal. I once spoke on this tragedy, and a nurse thanked me because she had just watched two young mothers die in the emergency room from cirrhosis of the liver. Alcohol has become a socially acceptable drug, and mentors need to help their mentees understand when they've stepped over the line into overuse or addiction. And today it's not just alchohol addiction, but also drugs. More on this topic is found in Chapter Thirteen.

> They should be examples of the good life
> (2:3b PHILLIPS)

- The *good life* doesn't mean material possessions, success, or pain-free living, but rather the amazing joy and peace we experience as followers of Jesus who receive God's goodness.

> so that the [spiritually] younger women may learn to love their husbands and their children, to be sensible and chaste, home-lovers, kind-hearted and willing to adapt themselves to their husbands (2:4–5 PHILLIPS)

- Spiritual mentoring focuses on being godly wives, mothers, and women uninfluenced by the world's ways. Notice also that Paul talks about wives loving husbands, not wives loving wives or husbands loving husbands. In an era in which homosexuality has become normalized by today's culture and gay marriage even legalized, Titus 2:1–8 substantiates God's plan for marriage to be only between a man and a woman. I also love how this translation describes wives keeping house as *home-lovers* who have kind and gentle hearts toward their husbands. Imagine the number of marriages a mentor might help heal and restore by teaching wives these verses!

> a good advertisement for the Christian faith.
> (2:5b PHILLIPS)

- We become a walking Christian testimony by the way we live our personal lives, raise our families, love our spouses, and help others find the peace only God can provide in a world quickly turning its back on God. We can make a difference, one woman at a time.

Verses 3–5 describe mentors who are positive godly role models—*not telling*, but *showing* mentees how to live as Christian women. Does this sound overwhelming? It shouldn't. This is the life God wants *every* Christian living. Someone helped us learn how to live as mature Christians, and now God wants us to pass on what we learned to a confused and vulnerable generation. The God of the Bible is still the God of the twenty-first century (Heb. 13:7–8). In Section Two, there are helpful tips for both mentors and mentees on the topics discussed in Titus 2, as well as many more issues specific to the seasons of a woman's life.

God called me into ministry and gave me a passion for spiritual mentoring. He imprinted on my heart an urgency that every Christian pass God's truths on to the next generation, so they will embrace his ways for themselves and experience an intimate personal relationship with Jesus, regardless of the culture—not just telling them *what* we believe, but sharing *why* we believe. Then we nurture and encourage them to develop knowledge, wisdom, and conviction to live for Christ, even in a world quickly turning to the ways of Satan.

In *Forsaken God?: Remembering the Goodness of God Our Culture Has Forgotten,* I stress that we must care about the next generation more than we care about ourselves. Our hearts need to break for confused young women who don't value their worth and virtue, as they look for sexual thrills, escape reality through drugs and alcohol, or become dissatisfied with their appearance or even their gender. We need to reach them with the message that they are daughters of the King before they let the world make them slaves of Satan.

Paul ends Titus 2 with the glorious results of helping mentees live godly lives while we wait for Christ's return:

> For the grace of God, which can save every man, has now become known, and it teaches us to have no more to do with godlessness or the desires of this world but to live, here and now, responsible, honourable and God-fearing lives. And while we live this life we hope and wait for the glorious appearance of the Great God and of Jesus Christ our saviour. For he gave himself for us all, that he might rescue us from all our evil ways and make for himself a people of his own, clean and pure, with our hearts set upon living a life that is good. (Titus 2:11–14 PHILLIPS)

Today there are Christians, and even pastors and churches, who say the Bible is irrelevant in today's culture, and some Christians have even embraced the culture's redefinition of marriage. The people of Jesus's day knew the Old Testament teachings about sin. Jesus didn't specifically say don't snort cocaine, don't engage in sex trafficking, don't murder unborn babies, or don't sell your body parts, so are they all okay today? The people of Jesus's day knew it was a sin to degrade their bodies, engage in sexual immorality and perversity, or murder . . . and these are still sins today. We need to help the next generation understand how to apply the *entire* Bible to living a moral, upright, and righteous life, because the world is neutralizing the definition of *sin*. We must remember Jesus's command, "Go now and leave your life of sin" (John 8:11).

THE STAGES OF MENTORING

CHAPTER SIX

*Mentoring requires no special talent or God-given quality.
All God asks is for us to take seriously the task of nurturing
and building up other women.*

—Lucibel "Lucki" Van Atta[1]

*Listen to advice and accept discipline,
and at the end you will be counted among the wise.*

—Proverbs 19:20

Every mentoring relationship will be different. There are no cookie-cutter, everyone-does-it-this-way mentoring rules. God puts two women together with unique gifts, personalities, goals, needs, and seasons. If they let him, God will guide in the direction he knows best for their mentoring relationship.

Some M&M's choose to do a Bible study or read a book and discuss it, and you'll find suggestions in the Resources for Specific Seasons section of the Appendix. Other M&M's will set different mentoring goals. *Always* keep God and his Word at the center of the relationship.

When Jesus left this earth, he told Christians our job was to continue his work on earth. We are to be like Jesus to everyone we meet and spread the good news of the Christian life to as many people as we can. What if you mentored twelve women in your lifetime, just as Jesus mentored his twelve disciples? Then your twelve mentees become mentors to twelve more women—that equals 144 M&M's. Extended out five more levels, the number of women in mentoring relationships from *you* mentoring one woman equals 2,985,984!

Look what you started. When the woman you invested time, effort, and energy in is ready to graduate and step forward as a role model to another woman . . . that's your "Well done, good and faithful servant." Even if not all your mentees become mentors, many will have a spiritual influence on others in their family, at work, neighbors, and friends. God will change many lives when you agree to mentor another woman or allow someone to mentor you.

I have story after story of marriages saved, families restored, relationships mended, husbands returning home after a separation or even filing for divorce, illnesses going into remission, depression turning to joy, husbands coming to the Lord, emotional and spiritual healing, mentees accepting Christ . . . just from two women committing to a mentoring relationship.

By representing "Jesus with skin on" to another woman—leading her to the one and only Counselor, Prince of Peace, and Divine Physician—you will accomplish more than any marriage counselor, attorney, or doctor. What does this take on your part? Time, energy, faith, and love, all of which you will receive back tenfold. Following are suggested steps in how to start a mentoring relationship and keep it healthy. The Appendix has additional suggestions for developing as a mentor and receiving blessings as a mentee.

Step One: Reaching Out

Someone has to make the initial contact to start the mentoring relationship. Maybe the mentor takes the first step. She has a desire to invest in another woman and is looking for someone to mentor, or she notices a woman going through a difficult season and offers to mentor her. Or the reverse may be true: a woman wanting help in a new season of her life reaches out to someone she admires and asks her to be a mentor. Every mentoring relationship will have a story of how God brought the M&M's together. The following is Jerre and Tara's story.

Jerre

My younger daughter, Kristy, was trying to renew her relationship with Christ at a time when I couldn't be there because of distance. Nancy was the answer to prayers that God bring a mentor into Kristy's life. Nancy did life with my child: Bible studies, prayer time, conferences, books . . . she was a spiritual mother. She mentored Kristy and got her back on her feet spiritually. I began asking the Lord to give me the opportunity to give back and invest in some young woman's life in the same way Nancy had invested in Kristy.

God answered my prayer when I was attending a First Place 4 Health class in our church. Tara, the young leader, expressed to the class a need for a job. I didn't know Tara well, but her need touched my heart, and I went up afterwards and offered my help in looking for a job opportunity.

Tara

I have two loving, praying Christian parents who faithfully took me to church, shared the Word of God, and kept God a priority in our home. I saw and heard them read the Bible and pray together for each of their children. I watched them seek God through job loss, hurts, and life's transitions. Life, however, was not perfect. I experienced losses that left me with questions and wounds, which I placed in a corner of my heart and dealt with when they surfaced in my life.

As a young newlywed, I asked older women whom I respected, and whose walk with the Lord I admired, to disciple me. Only a few responded positively, and most relationships only lasted the length of a Bible study. I was looking for something more—something deeper.

I first met Jerre while teaching a weight loss class at church. She was friendly and funny. As time progressed, she began to take an interest in my marriage, family, and relationship with the Lord.

Step Two: Getting to Know Each Other

If you don't already know each other, allow time to share your stories, especially your testimonies. The mentee might feel more comfortable sharing if the mentor tells her story first. If the mentee is reluctant or shy, don't force it. As you become better acquainted, and the mentee knows she can trust the mentor, her story will unfold as you get together more often.

Jerre

During my conversations with Tara, I learned she had three small boys and her husband was the Baptist collegiate ministry director on our local college campus. I knew she had a beautiful voice because I had heard her sing in church. I was chairman of our church women's ministry committee, and we needed a worship leader for our next women's ministry event. I asked Tara if she would consider it, and she eagerly accepted.

Then Tara joined a Bible study I was starting at church. A few weeks into the study, she called one afternoon and began sharing some things in her life that touched my heart because of similar issues we had dealt with in our own family.

Tara

Jerre took the initiative to get to know me, and I responded to the love she demonstrated by her interest in my thoughts, hurts, and life.

Step Three: Setting Boundaries and Guidelines

- Establish that the mentor won't have all the answers and won't make decisions for the mentee, but she will lead her to the sources of answers and righteous decision-making: Jesus, the Bible, and prayer.
- Decide the location, times, and length of meetings. If either person finds that getting together is taking more time than expected, she might be reluctant to meet as frequently.
- Discuss whether calling or texting is best. What are appropriate times for contact at home? At work? Weekends?

Creating mutually agreeable guidelines and boundaries helps prevent misunderstandings or infringement on personal space.

Jerre

I suggested we meet once a month for lunch for six months and then consider whether to continue. Either of us should feel free to walk away if the relationship wasn't beneficial. We began to meet and just talk, as we had agreed. I assured her she could tell me anything; I would keep her confidence. She could ask me anything; I would tell her the truth. I kept my promise. She was open and transparent about struggles in her life and marriage.

Tara

Jerre was willing to open her home and her heart to me and to others. I found a safe place for my heart to heal and flourish.

Step Four: Establishing Goals

Suggest you both pray about goals for the relationship and write down ideas to share when you get together. In what areas would the mentee like help and guidance, and how does the mentor feel she can help in those areas? Goals may change over the lifetime of the relationship, but you should have an initial focus when you start.

Jerre

We often laugh that a mentoring ministry probably wouldn't pair us together because our talents and gifts are so different. Tara is extremely musical, creative, and talented . . . I'm not. I'm athletic: I love to play tennis, golf, and bike. She's not. I love to cook and read. She's a reader and wanted to learn to cook, so we shared those interests. We both appreciated the differences and found common ground in Christ and our love for his Word and prayer. It was always my intent to point Tara to the sufficiency of Christ, his Word, and his perspective.

Tara

Eleven years ago, God took two women calling out to him for different needs and put us together to meet not only those needs, but also ones we didn't know we had. He united our hearts around his Word and his person. Jerre accepted all of me—gifts, failures, and secrets. She listened to, believed in, and prayed with me. We laughed and cried. She taught from the Word and exhorted me never to grow stagnant in my relationship with the Lord. I took a risk and trusted her because she enveloped me in grace and love the Lord gave her for me.

Always a Two-Way Relationship

I like how Heather Gillis, who shares her story in Chapter Thirteen, A Difficult Season, describes the mentor–mentee relationship as "symbiotic":

The mentor needs the mentee, and the mentee needs the mentor. I believe they both learn from each other and God uses their relationship to shape and mold them into his design for their life. Without a mentor, the mentee might never move forward in the calling God has for her life, and the mentor wouldn't experience the challenge to grow in her mentoring skills. Mentoring is such a beautiful relationship, requiring discernment of God's calling, will, patience, and wisdom.

Jerre

There is great joy and benefit in the reciprocal relationship of a younger–older woman Titus 2 friendship in Christ. Tara was one of the godliest and most mature young women I had ever met. She knew God well and loved his Word. I felt challenged to dig deeper and use his Word carefully in her life. God began to change me.

Tara

At first, I didn't know what I needed, but I do now. I needed the kindness of the Lord expressed in the love of another human being, who chose to give it by faith to another who chose to receive it by trust. The reciprocity of our unlikely friendship continues as we both encourage and challenge one another to grow in our relationship with the Lord.

Doing Life Together

Sometimes, but not always, mentoring relationships turn into lifelong friendships. Other times, they're just for a season and become fond memories of time spent together.

MENTORING FOR ALL SEASONS

Jerre

We liked each other and had a lot of fun together. It grew into an easy, casual Christ-centered friendship. Before long, I had twelve of Tara's peers in my living room meeting weekly for Bible study and prayer—they called us the "prayer posse." They were a group of young women who loved God, his Word, their families, and each other.

In the summer, we met weekly around our swimming pool with their children. It became a tradition for several years. Then God began to scatter them one by one as they moved away. I reminded them that the biblical use of the word "scattering" means sowing seeds, and it was now *their* responsibility to sow the seeds of what God had taught us together. They have sown in many different ways and places!

Tara

Jerre didn't show up to provide triage for my hurts; God placed her in my life during that season to rehabilitate my walk with the Lord. I'm more in love with him because of her.

The Mentee Becomes the Mentor

The heart of Titus 2 is one generation of believers teaching and training the next generation, who then in turn teach what they've learned to the next generation. There is no greater joy for a mentor than watching her mentee become the mentor.

Jerre

Tara moved away, but our story continues. The job she needed when we first met came through the opportunity to go back to school and get a graduate degree in counseling.

She is now a Christian counselor, disciples young women, teaches Bible studies, and still sings beautifully!

Keep Me Accountable

Whoever heeds life-giving correction
will be at home among the wise.

Those who disregard discipline despise themselves,
but the one who heeds correction gains understanding.
—Proverbs 15:31–32

If accountability is the focus or goal of the relationship, a mentor needs to carefully and thoroughly discuss accountability parameters:

- Specific areas where the mentee wants accountability
- Ways in which they *both agree* the mentor will keep her accountable

Here are some important points that will help avoid resistance and defensiveness:

- Mentees: Give your mentor permission to work with you on areas where you need help, and tell her how you want her to keep you accountable. Hearing someone point out areas of sin or necessary change is difficult. When a godly woman cares enough to risk your response, you have two choices: repent and change, or stubbornly dig in your heels and refuse. Your mentor can't do the hard work for you.
- Mentors: Ask the mentee to *agree* to your holding her accountable, and establish how and when this will take place. Change is hard and she may regress, but don't lose heart or determination. If you accept an accountability role, pray for courage to speak the truth kindly (see Eph. 4:15). Timing and inflection determine reception. Stay consistent,

and don't let things "slip by" in the hope they won't happen again—they probably will. You're one of the Holy Spirit's vessels working in your mentee's life.

Sometimes the mentee isn't aware she needs accountability, but after meeting for a while, the mentor may notice an area in the mentee's life that needs confronting. Esther shares how the Holy Spirit helped her keep her mentee accountable:

> Mary was a young married woman I mentored, and we went through a couple of books. I recognized she had a big issue that needed addressing. I tried talking to her directly and indirectly. Finally, led by the Spirit, I confronted her about the issue, and there was a breakthrough. Deeply desiring to be a woman of God, she was always grateful I was willing to risk our friendship and hold her accountable. I never would have known about this issue if we hadn't been in a one-on-one mentoring relationship.

It's wise for the mentor to remember that lecturing, scolding, and using Scripture as a weapon is not effective, as this anecdote reflects:

> As the older woman angrily berated the younger woman with Scripture, the younger woman, wearying of the lecture, displayed her discouragement. The older woman commented on the apparent disinterest of the younger woman who used to be so eager to learn. "I don't know what you want anymore."
>
> The younger woman replied, "In our time together all you've done is point out what's wrong with me. What do I want? I want to see Jesus in you!"

LIFE SEASONS OF MENTORS AND MENTEES (M&M'S)

Spiritual mentoring will seek to follow Jesus in content and style, in message and method, and in substance and form.
—Keith R. Anderson and Randy D. Reese[1]

I continue to be both a mentor and a mentee in all seasons of my life.
—Heather Gillis

And you should follow my example, just as I follow Christ's.
—1 Corinthians 11:1 (TLB)

INTRODUCTION TO SECTION TWO

As discussed in earlier chapters, mentoring covers a multitude of life seasons, including that of seekers and new believers. Churches often think they don't need a mentoring ministry because they have a discipleship ministry, but mentoring is so much more than that. Every woman, even a mature believer, needs a mentor when she's in a new season of life. I like to describe mentoring as an umbrella over *every* aspect of a woman's life—from seeking a relationship with God through maturing in her faith—and in her personal life seasons, from the tween years to the end of life.

Sometimes mentoring does involve discipling a new believer; other times, it's guiding a strong believer through a new life season. Mentoring encompasses guidance, accountability, spiritual growth, and friendship: one woman sharing her life experiences and her faith in God with another woman who could use help with her current life season.

Section Two explores mentoring during various seasons in a woman's life, *both* from the perspective of a mentor and a mentee. Many seasons of life overlap, and the same mentoring principles apply even when the details of the season may differ. As you go through a season, God expects you to reach back and mentor someone starting the same season you just came through, and God will provide someone to mentor you through your upcoming season. Keep your eyes, ears, and spirits open; look for signs he will send through circumstances and people. It might take time, so be patient, and pray for both a new mentor and a mentee.

In this part of the book, each chapter covers a particular season with several life experiences typically encountered in that season. Use the Table of Contents to find the season that best fits your situation as either the mentor or mentee; you may find it helpful to look at several different seasons' chapters, since we often experience more than one season at a time. The format of each chapter and the possible life experiences provided therein is as follows:

- **A Discussion Addressed to M&M's** opens each season and life experience.
- **Mentor Tips** and **Mentee Tips** offer specific suggestions and ideas for the mentor and the mentee.
- **God's Perspective: Search the Scriptures Together** addresses the importance of seeking God's answers to life's questions through the Bible and prayer. The Scriptures are to look up, read, discuss, and pray over together. Use them as a starting point, and find more on the topic together. *Always* have a Bible when you meet.
- **A Mentee Shares** and **A Mentor Shares** have amazing life-season stories and testimonies. Some names you might recognize as authors and speakers, others are M&M's, and all shared their stories with me to inspire and encourage you. Several use pseudonyms, but all are *true* stories, shared with permission.
- **M&M's from the Bible Share** point to biblical stories that reflect mentoring principles.
- **Let's Talk about It** are discussion questions for M&M's or for group settings or book clubs. (See the Guide for Using *Mentoring for All Seasons* in Mentoring Relationships, Bible Study/Small Groups, and Book Clubs, in the Appendix.)

The God's Perspective: Search the Scriptures Together sections are particularly important because the foremost role of mentoring is to help a mentee become familiar with her Bible: how to read, study, meditate on, memorize, and interact with Scripture on her own.

> So is my word that goes out from my mouth: It will not return to me empty, but will accomplish what I desire and achieve the purpose for which I sent it. (Isa. 55:11)

> I have hidden your word in my heart that I might not sin against you. (Ps. 119:11)

> For the word of God is alive and active. Sharper than any double-edged sword, it penetrates even to dividing soul and spirit, joints and marrow; it judges the thoughts and attitudes of the heart. (Heb. 4:12)

> I rejoice in your word like one who discovers a great treasure. (Ps. 119:162 NLT)

Mentors, be careful not to use Scripture as a big stick to beat the truth into your mentee. Instead, explore it together as a love letter from God depicting how he wants his followers to live as godly women. The mentor uses her own experiences as examples of how the Scriptures apply to her life when she follows them or the consequences when she rebels against them. Check the Appendix for ways to look up more verses on a particular topic.

Also in the Appendix are Resources for Specific Seasons and Life Experiences, where you will find suggested books to read together, or for research, and mentoring Bible studies to study together, along with additional tips on mentoring relationships, both as a mentor and mentee.

———————————————— ⌒ ————————————————

Tricia Goyer has met for twelve years with a group of other bestselling authors for a brainstorming retreat. She wrote the following comment on Facebook during this year's retreat. I asked to share it because she describes the joys of mentoring and the call to be a mentor during all seasons of life.

> Truly, the best part of this retreat is walking through life with these women. They are humble God-lovers who model what it means to seek and serve God. They invite me to watch their lives and imitate their faith. Each of them has gone through trials, but their faith in God hasn't wavered. They give and they love even in the midst of hard things.
>
> By watching and being loved by them, I've discovered Christian unity. I've also understood the power of grace in everyday life—giving it and receiving it. I'm the youngster of this group, and learning from these women has reminded me of the importance of reaching behind and spending time with those younger than me. Not just receiving; giving, too.
>
> If you don't have God-loving Christian women in your life, pray and ask God to guide you to them. Then go where they are: church, Bible study groups, Christian women's or writers' groups, MOPS, etc. It's hard to step out and be vulnerable, but it's so worth breaking down those walls. Mentoring is truly one way each of us can walk out Scripture in everyday lives: Hebrews 13:7, "Remember your leaders, who spoke the word of God to you. Consider the outcome of their way of life and imitate their faith." I'm a better wife, mother, writer, and friend because I've learned to imitate the faith of amazing women. If you seek God for this in your life too, He will provide in amazing ways.

CHAPTER SEVEN

SEEKER OR NEW BELIEVER SEASON

I've told my mentor, God put her in my life at the beginning of my walk with him because he knew the struggles I'd have—which she knew personally—and yet she clung to him. I owe her my marriage, my ministry, and who I have become by God's grace.

—Poppy Smith

For God so loved the world that he gave his one and only Son, that whoever believes in him shall not perish but have eternal life.

—John 3:16

Mentees aren't always Christians. They just might want to learn more about the Christian faith—something a mentor should know in the beginning of the mentoring relationship. Before the mentor can start applying spiritual principles to the mentee's life, she first must discover where her mentee is spiritually.

Maybe she's a seeker who isn't sure she even wants to become a Christian, but she *does* want information without the pressure of having to make a decision. These can be sweet times as a mentor watches the truth of God's Word unfold in her mentee's life, or they can be disparaging times if her heart remains hardened.

Perhaps you're a seeker mentee with questions or a new Christian mentee needing spiritual guidance: this is the most important season in your life. As you learn what it means to be a Christian, you can begin to see how to apply faith to life circumstances. People seek the Lord as their Savior at all ages. We often think of new believers as chronologically young, but many accept Jesus into their heart later in life and desperately need mentoring.

The mentor, while spiritually older, may be chronologically younger than the new believer mentee. Regardless of age, we all start out in our Christian walk needing to learn the basics of Christianity before we can digest and understand the depths of spiritual food, God's Word, the bread of life (John 6:35). The Bible also says that a new believer must become like a child, eager to learn and mature in her spiritual knowledge and life application.

Just like children need nurturing and teaching, so do new believers. One of the big voids in the church is lack of follow-up with new believers. They're often given a Bible, or told to buy one, and then advised to read the Gospel of John, join a church, and live as a Christian . . . even though they have no idea what a Christian lives like.

Often new believers, at any age, won't join Bible studies or come to small groups or Sunday school, because they're embarrassed of what they don't know—especially if they're older. The new believer can feel safe to ask questions one on one with a trusted mentor rather than in front of a group. Or the mentor can attend a Bible study or small group with her mentee.

Other times, the mentee has backslidden or become stale in her faith and is seeking a renewal and refreshing in her relationship with the Lord and how to apply her faith to life's challenges. Oswald Chambers wrote,

> Our work is not to save souls, but to disciple them. Salvation and sanctification are the work of God's sovereign grace, and our work as His disciples is to disciple others' lives until they are totally yielded to God. . . . As workers for God, we must reproduce our own kind spiritually, and those lives will be God's testimony to us as His

workers. God brings us up to a standard of life through His grace, and we are responsible for reproducing that same standard in others.[1]

Mentor Tips ....

In any mentoring relationship, let the mentee progress at a comfortable speed. Don't put pressure on yourself to convert a seeker, or push the new believer too hard. Ask specific questions to discover where the mentee is spiritually. A Bible study is premature if your mentee is still a seeker. Maybe your entire mentoring time will be answering questions, reading a book together like *The Case for Christ*, and moving her closer to becoming a believer. Let the Holy Spirit guide you.

Whether your mentee is a seeker, is a new believer, or wants to rededicate her life, share your testimony of accepting Jesus into your heart. There was a time in your life when you were a seeker too. What helped you move from seeker to new believer to maturing spiritually?

If your mentee is a new believer, ask if she's familiar with the Bible and knows how to look up scriptural passages. If she doesn't have a Bible, help her select one. Talk about how to have a quiet time. Explain the value of prayer and how it is simply a conversation with God. If your church has a new believers' class, offer to attend with her.

You probably won't know the answers to all her questions, so promise to find the answers and then follow through on your promise. Beware of lapsing into Christianese—"the blood," "your walk," "spiritual warfare." She can learn the meaning of these terms later. For now, use simple, common words that are easy to understand. You have an infant who needs formula and basics until she's ready to mature to solid food. Or you may even have a spiritual embryo waiting to be born again. If you get the opportunity, you can use the Seeker Question or have your mentee pray the Salvation Prayer (which can also be used as a rededication prayer), found in the Appendix.

Mentee Tips ....

Whether just curious about Christianity or a new believer, having a mentor is an awesome opportunity to learn how to apply the Bible's teachings to your daily life. Be a humble and diligent learner, but feel free to ask questions. Don't feel intimidated. This is your opportunity to spend time with someone who can help you study and understand more about what it means to be a Christian. Use this time wisely and show your appreciation to the woman God has chosen to guide you in this significant season of your faith journey.

God's Perspective: Search the Scriptures Together

God has much to say about helping seekers and new believers mature spiritually so someday they can be mentors and teachers themselves. He also rebukes any of us who refuse to grow in his Word and his ways. See the following verses:

- We all start out as babes in Christ—Luke 18:15–17; Heb. 5:13–14
- God wants us to be receptive to learning his ways— Ps. 25:4–5, 25:9
- God wants mentors to be his teachers to new believers— Ps. 32:8
- Believers must be born again—John 3:3, 6:29; 1 Pet. 1:23
- Not receiving Jesus as your Savior is rejecting him— John 3:36, 12:48; 1 Thess. 4:8

A Mentee Shares—Rosalie

Our pastor asked Doris to disciple and mentor me. At forty-five, I was a new Christian and my father had just died. I was struggling with grief and messy relationships with my four children, and I was trying to interact well with an ex-husband and my current husband. I needed more than a discipler; I needed a friend who understood my pain and weaknesses. I wanted a comforter first—an encourager—and then a teacher.

I met Doris for the first time in the church parking lot and immediately sensed her friendliness and sincerity. We agreed to meet once a week, and those times over the course of two years were precious. Our friendship grew as she taught me about God's Word, Jesus's love, and leaning on him to meet my emotional, physical, and spiritual needs.

Doris was more than a close friend and mentor; she was an encouraging cheerleader, inspiring me to victory through Christ when I encountered life's battles. When she felt I was ready to spread my wings spiritually, Doris urged me to use my spiritual gift of leadership to start a Bible study group for women struggling with tough circumstances.

A Mentor Shares—*Rosalie*

Starting a small group for women gave me a sense of purpose. One of the women was struggling with relationship issues with her husband. On New Year's Day, Laura appeared at my door in tears. She wanted an older woman mentor who understood her crisis, and she chose me. Wow! I didn't see that coming, but I was thrilled. When I agreed to mentor Laura, God challenged me to become a Titus 2 woman. We met weekly for a Bible study on how the Lord heals our hurts. With lots of prayer and forgiveness, she resolved her relationship issues with her husband. Our mentoring relationship enriched both our lives: I also learned how to be a better wife and mother.

M&M's *from* the Bible Share—Naomi and Ruth

The story of Naomi and Ruth in the Book of Ruth occurred during their culture's dark period of sin, idolatry, violence, lawlessness, disobedience, and chaos. "Everyone did as he saw fit" (Judg. 17:6, 21:25)—much like our culture today.

Ruth grew up in Moab, a pagan society, where Naomi moved with her husband and two sons. Ruth married one of Naomi's sons and lived with Naomi for ten years. Naomi worshipped God and was a godly mentor and role model for Moabite Ruth to admire and emulate. Ruth was a seeker. Drawn to the light she saw in Naomi, Ruth was eager to know more about Naomi's God.

When both their husbands died and Naomi decided to go back home to Bethlehem, mentee Ruth professed her faith:

"Don't urge me to leave you or to turn back from you. Where you go I will go, and where you stay I will stay. Your people will be my people and your God my God. Where you die I will die, and there I will be buried. May the LORD deal with me, be it ever so severely, if even death separates you and me." When Naomi realized Ruth was determined to go with her, she stopped urging her. (Ruth 1:16–18)

Let's Talk about It

1. Who mentored you from a seeker to becoming a believer? What is your testimony?
2. How could the term "seeker sensitive" apply to a mentoring relationship?
3. Why is it so important for new believers to have a mentor?
4. Read the Book of Ruth. (It's only four chapters.) How did Naomi and Ruth have a mentoring relationship?

CHAPTER EIGHT

TWEEN AND TEEN SEASON

Can you hear a host of teen girls crying, asking, and waiting for your help and guidance? Right now think of a young woman, a tween or a teen, you might know. She may be your daughter, your niece, or just a young girl you're acquainted with. You could be the person in her life to dust off her tiara, place it on her head, and help her see herself as God sees her—a person valued and loved. And you could do this for many girls, moving a multitude of young women into a healthy, whole, and wholesome future as adult women who make a difference for their generation.

—Pam Farrel and Doreen Hanna[1]

Come, my children, listen to me;
I will teach you the fear of the Lord.

—Psalm 34:11

If we don't teach our children to follow Christ, the world will teach them not to.

Such a sad reality . . . and if spiritually older women don't reach out to teach and train the younger generations, those children are left to figure things out on their own while listening to the liberal barrage of worldly advice derailing them from every direction—media, social media, movies, TV, schools, friends, the community. If they don't hear the ageless truths of God, they easily succumb to the timeless lies of Satan. Today's mantra, supported by liberals and the secular culture and media, is "truth is overrated, and honesty is relative to whatever you think truth is for you." Yet God gave us a proven way to prevent this moral decay in our society. We could have avoided much of the evil happening in the world if Christians and the church had been willing to invest in spiritually mentoring the next generations and maintaining an active voice in government: "But this is what you must do: Tell the truth to each other. Render verdicts in your courts that are just and that lead to peace" (Zech. 8:16 NLT).

Our first mentoring responsibility is to our children. If you have daughters, are you the woman today you want your daughter to become? One of my friends, who became a Christian later in life, said her daughter told her, "I don't want to be the woman you were when I was growing up. I want to be the woman you are today!" Our daughters are watching; we're their closest role model—good or bad. Like I was to Kristen, my first mentee—who I mentioned in the Introduction—sometimes daughters need a mentor besides Mom:

> During a mother-daughter chat with my daughter, Michelle, I mentioned my desire to tell her sister, Kim, a vital truth relevant to Kim's spiritual growth as a new Christian. Michelle's response was wise, but hard for me to hear: "It's probably better that Kim hears this from someone else. You know kids always listen more to advice from women other than their mom. We don't think Mom can be objective when it comes to us."
>
> Oh, did these words sting! I knew it was true because I had a similar reaction to my mom's advice, and it made her so mad. I would come home with some great revelation my friend's mom had said, and my mom would admonish me: "I said the same thing to you!"
>
> Often, we feel our moms are prejudiced and biased when it comes to us. Or we fear they have their own agenda and motives, so we seek out someone whom we feel will give us uncensored advice and answers to our questions.[2]

Praise God there are many dedicated Sunday school teachers and vibrant youth ministries, but as young people mature and start making their own decisions, the church often backs away when needed the most. Instead of helping young people confront the difficult issues they deal with today, the church becomes shy and reserved about discussing real-world issues. Dr. Owen Strachan, assistant professor of Christian theology and church history at the Southern Baptist Theological Seminary in Louisville, Kentucky, and president of the Council of Biblical Manhood and Womanhood warns:

> *We will minister to a people who are suffering the effects of rampant sin.* There will be profound moral and spiritual consequences of the new sexual secularism. America is in the midst of a spiritual un-awakening. In everyday terms, this means that human suffering in America will increase. Children will be less protected. Families will feel pressure to pull apart. Marriages will prove harder to sustain. Lostness, the chief form of suffering in this world, will spread.
>
> The witness of God on the human heart will be silenced by a culture that approves of what we naturally know is wicked and damaging. To isolate just one issue, as transgender identity spreads and is accepted, little boys and girls who years ago would have received sound counsel to inhabit their God-given bodies will instead be encouraged to undergo drastic surgery. They will experience profound confusion as a result and will be—by some estimates—twenty times more likely to commit suicide than their peers. This is just one illustration of the baleful effects of the forces that now bully our body politic into conformity to anti-wisdom and anti-truth.[3]

I did a survey on Facebook asking how many in women's ministry would welcome young girls, starting around age fifteen, to their events. The majority said absolutely, and even younger girls would be welcome. One woman summarized what many championed:

> Young girls deal with "in-your-face" issues more than ever before. I would definitely open up women's ministry events to them. I work in schools and girls are HUNGRY and looking for reasons to remain pure. They're searching for boundaries and hoping women will lead and mentor them.

Yet still far too many churches don't include tweens and teens in women's ministry events, which breaks my heart. The main reason I hear is that moms want to get away from the responsibilities of home without their children. While I agree today's busy moms need a getaway, this shouldn't be the sole purpose of a church-sponsored event. Where else will young girls learn how to live pure and holy lives if not in the church?

I pray families are mentoring their girls, but looking at our culture today . . . it isn't happening as it should. And what about the girls who don't have believing parents? Girls face worldly choices and temptations at young ages, and we need to reach them *before* they make unhealthy choices they will live with for the rest of their lives. For those dear girls who have already made regrettable choices, we need to introduce them to our gracious, loving, and forgiving heavenly Father.

Mentor Tips ....

Be cognizant of possible problem issues:

- If you notice troubling areas, discuss them with the mentee's parents and let her know you will be doing so.
- If there's abuse or problems at home, talk with your pastor as to how to proceed.

- This season is ripe for cliques, "mean girls," and bullying. Be sensitive if your mentee is experiencing any of these or if she is participating in them.
- Puberty and adolescence can be a time of gender confusion, or it might even be considered trendy to explore. If you see any signs, go to Chapter Thirteen, Gender Identity Issues and Sexual Integrity.

While young girls often are more open with a "spiritual mom" than with their own mom, you still must have a conversation with your mentee's mom letting her know her daughter asked you to mentor her, and you'll be mentoring from a spiritual perspective. You need Mom's permission. Assure Mom you'll keep her in the loop. Also, discuss with the mentee and Mom that you must tell Mom anything you feel she needs to know or anything she asks about, and the mentee will know what you share with Mom.

Never forget you aren't the parent. Even if you don't agree, you must cooperate with the parents' choices, unless harmful for the child (then you may need to call authorities). Never talk badly about a parent. Your role is to help this young girl grow close to her heavenly Father, not build a wedge between her and her earthly parents.

Also, have a conversation with your children. Be especially sensitive to daughters' jealousy or unwillingness to share you. Use their feelings as an opportunity to talk about the value of mentoring, and encourage them to find a spiritual mother. Explain the term "spiritual mother" and the reasons you chose to mentor another young girl. It might be beneficial to invite the mentee to some family functions so the girls can meet.

If friction continues in your home, wait until your daughters are out of the house and mentor a woman older than your daughters' ages. Your own daughters are your first mentoring priority.

Never think a girl is too young to do a Bible study or read a book together. At age nine, my granddaughter, Katelyn, asked if she could have one of my books for Easter. I gave her *Face-to-Face with Mary and Martha: Sisters in Christ*. Even though I didn't write this Bible study specifically for young girls, we did the study together. What a joy to watch Katelyn look up the scriptural readings in her Bible, answer the questions, and discuss how to apply the lessons to her young life.

Then one day her younger sister, seven-year-old Sienna, asked to join Katelyn and me for our Bible study. Sienna is a good example of how to include Mom in the mentoring loop. On the way to do our study over lunch, Sienna said she came with us because she wanted to accept Jesus into her heart. Wow! What a blessed surprise. When we got to the restaurant, I called Mommy to see if she wanted me to pray with Sienna or if she would rather be present. Mommy said if Sienna was ready, I should go ahead. Now I'm enjoying the "spiritual mother" role with both my granddaughters. We have sweet discussions as we look up verses together in their Bibles and answer the study questions. When we can't meet in person, we do our study via Skype.

Pray for God to make you aware of tweens and teens needing a mentor: maybe a young girl at church whose parents don't attend church. I was that young girl, and I'm a believer today because caring women at church invited me to a church camp, where I accepted Jesus as my Lord and Savior.

Or perhaps like Crystal Bowman, who prayed God would use her in a ministry where she could still care for her young children, God will give you an opportunity to work with girls in your community. Sometimes at this age, girls are more comfortable in a group setting.

One day I got a call from a family acquaintance, Tim, the Youth for Christ director who ran a program at our local high school. "I don't know why," he said, "but your name keeps coming to my mind. I have a small group of teenage girls who want to have a Bible study. We can't have it at school, and I have no one to lead."

"They can meet at my house, and I'll lead it." Then I shared how I'd been praying for God to give me a ministry, and this was the perfect answer to prayer!

For a school year, four emotional and energetic teen girls brought joy, laughter, and drama into my home for two hours every Monday afternoon, while we did a Bible lesson with lots of good discussion. I hired a "mama's helper" to play with my young boys.

We often got off topic, which I felt was the Holy Spirit leading to God's agenda rather than mine. We talked about God, boys, parents, marriage, and friends. We prayed, and sometimes cried, together. Often, one or two would help me make dinner. I soon began to use them as babysitters. One became a lifelong friend, and we've kept in touch for thirty years.

Mentee Tips ....

Remember the following regarding your mentor:

- She isn't your mom, but she can be a "spiritual mom."
- She will need to meet your parents or guardian and get their approval.
- She will tell your parents if you do something dangerous, harmful, or illegal.
- She won't have all the answers to your questions, but she will do research and always guide you to God and the Bible for answers.

God's Perspective: Search the Scriptures Together

In the family of God—our church and Christian community—we should consider the children of the church *our* children in terms of their spiritual nurturing and care. Most parents welcome help in raising their children to be believers who love the Lord and assistance in keeping them accountable during formative years. We're in this together—raising the next generation to love and reverence God. So many verses affirm this call to Christians, as we looked at in Section One. Here are a few more.

- God tells us to mentor children—Prov. 20:11, 22:6; Isa. 38:19, 54:13

When she has tough questions, or opens up about temptations and struggles, use the Bible to affirm what God wants.

- If tempted to become sexually active, God says to flee from sexual sin—1 Cor. 6:12–14, 6:18; 1 Thess. 4:2–6
- If tempted to try drugs, alcohol, cutting, body alternations, or smoking—Matt. 6:13
- Jesus combated temptation by quoting Scripture— Matt. 4:1–11; Mark 14:38; Luke 11:4; 1 Cor. 10:13

Remind her that any kind of sex outside the context of marriage between a man and a woman is sexual sin, and God created us male *or* female. Let her know that Satan, the father of lies (John 8:44), is the one telling her homosexuality or sexual sin is no big deal today. Also refer to the Gender Identity Issues and Sexual Integrity season in Chapter Thirteen.

- Questions about gender identity—Gen. 1:27, 5:2
- Homosexuality—1 Tim. 1:9–11
- Peer pressure—Rom. 12:2; 1 Pet. 1:13–16

A Mentee Shares—*Julie*

Shortly after the Lord saved me in high school, the wife of the Young Life director at my school befriended me. We would talk on the phone for long stretches of time. I didn't realize then, but it was a form of mentoring. Though I don't remember this gracious woman ever giving advice or input on how to live, she helped bond my relationship to Christ. A grown woman reached down into my high-school-girl world and simply listened. Thinking back, she was my first key mentoring experience after receiving the Lord.

A Mentee Shares—*Trudy Samsill*

I met my God-sent mentor during my early teens. Across the aisles at church, I always admired her sweet, approachable face, but I was too insecure to do more than a swift "Good morning, Miss Laura." Then one day, she wanted to talk to *me* about possibly babysitting her son. She invited me to her home to discuss the details of the babysitting job.

I got the job, and quickly this precious lady—only fourteen years older than me—accepted, loved, and believed in me, a skinny, unsure, questioning girl. Wanting to enter my world, Laura always asked heart-searching questions in a way to help me discover who I was.

> *What's your favorite color?* We had this color when we painted.

> *What food do you like?* A dish we would prepare together in the future.

> *Have you ever read this author?* If not, she'd get a copy of the author's books.

> *What are your dreams?* I had to search deep inside.

> *What do you want to do when you're older?* More searching.

I expressed to her freshly discovered dreams, fears, and hidden self-doubts I was afraid to admit even to myself. On my birthday, she gave me a poster with a ballerina and these words: "If you can imagine it, you can achieve it. If you can dream it, you can become it." My mentor drove this message home to my young floundering heart.

Reflecting on the many things Laura taught me in word and deed, some have had a deep impact on my life and on how I mentor:

- Slowly sip hot tea with honey, served in pretty teacups, while having long talks with your companion.
- I hear her as I ask my daughter and other young women the questions Laura asked me: "What do you daydream about?" or "How's your heart?"
- When self-doubt and fears assault, she would always reassure, "You can do this! Believe in the God who created you and believe in yourself! Keep dreaming!"

Laura wrote a review on my first Amazon ebook, *Glass Marbles*. We didn't know these would be her last words ever communicated to me.

> *By Laura: When I read a story, the first thing I look for is a reason to care about the characters. I was immediately interested in this story, the plot idea is direct and doesn't wander. The only thing I wanted was MORE! I hope Trudy will write a sequel so I can find out what happens in the next months. Nicely done.*

Today, I still think of her, especially when I write or mentor younger women. God wove her influence into the fabric of who I am and how I touch others. Caring for, listening to, encouraging, and supporting a younger woman are traits my wonderful mentor taught me. As Laura did when she sought me out and entered my world, there's someone out there for me, for you, to proactively influence through the beautiful ministry of mentoring. Find your mentee, like my mentor found me. She needs what you have to share with her!

A Mentor Shares—*Pamela*

My son dated Brooke when he was a sophomore in high school. Brooke's grandpa (her sole male influence) died, and she started having severe emotional issues affecting her schoolwork. Brooke's single mom was also grieving her father, while trying to work and raise Brooke. Mom and I started talking and became good friends. I offered to help with Brooke if Mom needed me to pick her up after school, get her to doctor's appointments, whatever I could do.

I was another adult woman for Brooke to turn to for help, who listened to her, took her shopping and to movies, and just hung out with her. I always tried to add an element of fun. I mentored her the next three years of high school. Often, she left school in tears because of mean bullying girls, and I went to bat for Brooke with teachers or others at school. There was a time when her mom put her on medication; I didn't agree, but I didn't fight Mom.

Brooke graduated high school after playing *every* lead female part in school plays. I was there for most performances. She went on to a university and grew into a beautiful, poised young woman. She is now studying opera at a conservatory in Vienna and has found the love of her life. I consider it an honor and privilege to be a part of Brooke's life. Because I reached out to a hurting child, I have a lifelong connection to two of the most important people in my life.

A Mentor Shares—*Sharron*

I asked our church high school pastor if there were any high school girls looking for a deeper walk with God. Six girls had recently approached him about forming this type of a group. I had the privilege of mentoring freshman through senior high school girls in a discipleship group for seven years before moving on to mentoring college women.

Years later, I received a text from a former mentee, now married with children and living in another state: "At Christmas, I shared the gospel with my aunt [who lives near me]. I'd love to have someone follow up." After praying, I called and invited her aunt to a movie and lunch. When the door opened, we had a meaningful discussion about what it means to have a relationship with God.

Had I not followed God's calling to mentor high school girls, I'd have missed the opportunity to share God with someone who doesn't know him. My mentee and I have become fellow *seed planters* in her aunt's life.

M&M's *from* the Bible Share

In Luke 1:26–56, Mary (mother of Jesus) was a young teenager when the angel Gabriel told her she would become the mother of the Messiah. In ancient Israel, girls often married and had children in their tween/ teenage years, so this wasn't so unusual. But a virgin having a baby was miraculous. The next part of Gabriel's message was key: Mary should go visit her relative Elizabeth (mother of John the Baptist), in her eighties, who was also miraculously pregnant. God was establishing a mentoring relationship between teenage Mary and elderly Elizabeth.

Mary hurried off to visit Elizabeth instead of staying home with her own mom. Perhaps Mom didn't understand or believe Mary's story, or she was in shock, judgment, or fear for Mary's safety. Maybe she rejected Mary or intuitively recognized that Elizabeth could better relate to Mary's circumstances. They also might have agreed Mary would be a comfort and help to Elizabeth in her last months of pregnancy.

Let's Talk about It

1. Have you had the opportunity to mentor a teenager? Did you have a mentor or spiritual mom when you were a teenager?
2. Why do you think teenagers often talk to someone besides their parents about sensitive issues?
3. What are the mentoring advantages of including teens in women's ministry?
4. What are the issues facing tweens and teens today?

YOUNG ADULT SEASON

My mentor is always straight up with me. Cries with me. Laughs with me. Won't let me off the hook. Holds me to who she believes I am becoming. Says the hard things. Keeps no record of wrongs. Challenges and exhorts me. Priceless to me. #lifers #ineveryseason

—Amy

*He decreed statutes for Jacob and established the law in Israel,
which he commanded our ancestors to teach their children,
so the next generation would know them, even the children yet to be born,
and they in turn would tell their children.*

—Psalm 78:5–6

In the Introduction, I told the story of hearing God's call to "Feed my sheep" and of the God-ordained encounter with Pastor Brad, the Saddleback Church pastor to young adults, which launched the Woman to Woman Mentoring Ministry. As I took the steps to start the mentoring ministry at Saddleback, Pastor Brad requested I first speak with his group.

I learned how eager the young women in this young adults group were for spiritually older women to spend time with them. They had so many questions about venturing out into the world away from home and parents. Churches often overlook this impressionable age group. No longer considered "youth," the church often leaves them to stumble into adulthood on their own during a crucial season of making choices and decisions that will influence the rest of their lives. Today's millennials are accepting the new "progressive Christianity"—a form of atheism touting the Bible as an irrelevant ancient book, and right or wrong is determined by each person's own interpretation and experience. Statistics of this age group leaving the church are alarming:

- A study from LifeWay Research reveals 70 percent of young adults ages twenty-three to thirty stopped attending church regularly for at least a year between the ages of eighteen and twenty-two. Some listed "life-change" issues as a reason: "I moved to college and stopped attending church" (25 percent) and "Work responsibilities prevented me from attending" (23 percent). Others "simply wanted a break from church" (27 percent).
- Young adults who stay in church through the ages of eighteen through twenty-two see the relevance, benefits, and purpose of the church now and for their future: "Church was a vital part of my relationship with God" (65 percent), and "I wanted the church to help guide my decisions in everyday life" (58 percent).[1]

Many of today's colleges permeate young minds with liberalism and no accountability to God's timeless truths. Thrown into a world with lax or no moral codes, and probable attacks on their Christian beliefs, many young collegiate Christians *crumble* rather than *crusade* for their faith.

If the young women enter the work world, few businesses champion, appreciate, or practice Christian values and ethics. Young adulthood is the time when those in serious dating relationships contemplate marriage. Is anyone asking these young women if their future husband is a Christian? Do they share the same faith? Are they sexually tempted, pressured, or already crossing the line sexually?

This is a crossroads season where faith meets real life. Eager to be their own boss, they enter a world increasingly hostile to Christians. Will they have the courage to stick with their beliefs and God's ways, or will they succumb to culture's ways? These young adults need a caring, praying mentor to help them stay faithful to their Christian beliefs and lifestyles.

Not every young woman has a Christian mother or even a loving mother. Many find themselves spiritually alone as the only Christian in their family or circle of friends, or physically alone living far away from family. Some issues are difficult to discuss with Mom. Where are the mentors who are up for this challenge of mentoring these young adult women?

Mentor Tips ....

Everyone anticipates this long-awaited season of testing independence—finally, the right to make decisions away from family influence and parental constraints! These young women usually feel wise and competent, and they often resent anyone telling them what to do or how to do it. However, unwise use of newfound freedoms can quickly lead to disillusioned and derailed young women.

If times have changed dramatically since you were this age, *research* and *respect* this season. Avoid alienating your mentee or making her feel foolish or naïve. Don't categorize her as a "millennial" or "Gen X, Y, or Z." She wants recognition as God's unique creation.

The younger generation has grown up in a culture banning God, Jesus, prayer, and the Bible from schools, hospitals, and many places in the public square. They don't know that these were Christian rights and freedoms until a generation ago. Your mentee's norm is people being afraid to say "Merry Christmas" or labeled "haters" for calling sin a sin. So educate her on biblical and American history of forsaking and rejecting God versus times of great revival and repentance. Encourage her to follow God's ways, not the world's ways, and help her understand the difference between the two.

Some spiritually older women mistakenly think this age group isn't interested in mentoring, but in my experience, they're desperately crying out for help and guidance. They want a mentor who will

- Walk beside, not in front of them
- Listen before offering opinions
- Be open and vulnerable
- Share personal difficulties and failures from their experiences at this age
- Understand and appreciate the communication tools this age group uses
- Not talk down or treat them like children
- Be authentic and genuine in her faith
- Love and live the Christian life joyfully
- Not condemn them, but not condone ungodly behavior
- Be sensitive that they may have already made mistakes and need to feel God's forgiveness, grace, and encouragement not to repeat them again

Check the Table of Contents for other life seasons that might be applicable to your mentee, and Chapter Thirteen for Abuse, Addiction, Criminal Activities, Gender Identity Issues, and Sexual Integrity, and Post-Abortion Recovery.

Mentee Tips

To make the most out of your time with your mentor, try to do the following.

- Be open and honest.
- Let her help and guide you to what God would have you do.
- Give her grace. She may not understand your world entirely; but she does understand God's world and his Word.
- Honor her time and effort.
- Have a teachable spirit.
- Be grateful God loves you so much he brought this woman into your life to shed some light on these transition years.

God's Perspective: Search the Scriptures Together

This season of life can encounter many of the same issues and temptations as the tween and teen season, so refer to Chapter Eight for scriptural passages on sexual, drug, alcohol, and smoking temptations; gender identity issues; same-sex attraction; and peer pressure. Here are a few additional areas you might encounter with this season:

- Dating or considering marriage—2 Cor. 6:14
- Living together, hooking up, or sex outside of marriage; sex is exclusive to marriage regardless of the world or some "Christians" trying to normalize sexual sin—1 Cor. 7:2–3
- Seeking God's will for career choices, or any choice— Ps. 25:5, 31:3
- Listening to peers rather than seeking sage wisdom— 2 Chron. 10:8

A Mentee Shares—*Amy*

I met Heather my freshman year of college. She was two years older, my R.A. (floor mom), and quickly became a trusted confidant, close friend, encourager, and mentor. We have so much in common: music, Jesus, and our love for worship. Eventually, we became prayer partners and walked with each other through relationships, helped process and heal from painful breakups, and extended truth and accountability.

Our lives have woven together in many ways—from singing in each other's weddings to now twenty years later, still leading worship together. Six weeks after my first child was born, Heather and her husband adopted their first baby. Together we shared the challenges and joys of being first-time parents, encouraging each other every step of the way. I've moved across the country several times, but God has allowed us to stay deeply connected.

Heather is a steadfast and loyal friend and always speaks God's truth over my life. She never lets me get away with settling for less than the pursuit of God's very best. She has wept with me and celebrated my victories as if they were her own. I can barely articulate the gift of a mentor friend like this. I have no birth sister, but she's my sister: one of life's greatest and sweetest gifts.

A Mentee Shares—Kathy

I prayed for God to bring the perfect mentor. I'd been dating Darren and we were considering marriage. I wanted a godly woman to help navigate this decision and transition into marriage. Then I met Penny at a women's retreat, where she was leading a workshop. I went up to her afterwards and asked if we could chat. Later that evening, I asked her to mentor me. My friend Ginny attended Penny's workshop also, and she too was looking for a mentor. We both felt God saying, "Penny is your girl!"

The first time we met at Penny's house, we instantly felt loved and welcome. We spent many nights "at her feet" listening to her wisdom. She shared the times she got it right . . . and the times she didn't. Penny was open, honest, and transparent. She *always* pointed us to Jesus and encouraged us to seek him first. When we were together, the Holy Spirit guided our conversations, creating an atmosphere that made it easy to share, learn, and grow. I loved how we could ask Penny *anything*, and she answered with his grace and wisdom.

I grew tremendously in my relationship with God. Penny taught me how to pray and worship him. I also learned about hospitality and servanthood: two of Penny's gifts! When Penny moved out of state, I felt a part of me was missing. I thank God for the five glorious years we spent together learning, listening, and praying.

A Mentee Shares—*Ginny*

It was a season of new beginnings when Kathy, Penny, and I started meeting. I was a new Christian—a little over a year—planning my wedding. When we met weekly, it was a safe place to share questions, thoughts, fears, and joys, without judgment. Penny opened up her home and her life, sharing her stories of struggles with marriage and family. She was real. I felt like a part of her family. We studied Jesus through the Bible and Bible studies, but she shared Jesus mostly by just *loving* and *guiding* me to him! I will always have the memories of the special times we shared together.

A Mentor Shares—*Penelope "Penny" Carlevato*

I am blessed with my mentor Bobette, who prays for me, steers me in the right way, and encouraged me in starting Penelope's Tea Time Ministry. I felt it was time to share my experiences, good and bad, with young women coming up behind me. Our church had a mentoring program, so I decided to jump in. What an experience! I met with three different girls and didn't click with any of them. I prayed and told the Lord if he wanted me to mentor, he would have to bring them to me.

The next week, I was leading a workshop at our women's retreat. After the session, a young woman (Kathy) came up and wanted to talk. When we met, she asked if I would mentor her. We were both nurses, so I wanted to say yes. I knew this was probably my answer to prayer, but I also knew I should take time to pray.

After several days, I knew Kathy was the gal I was to mentor. She also asked if she could bring her friend Ginny. This began a long and lovely relationship. Several other young women came to our weekly get-togethers. Some stayed for a few months, and some for a year, but Kathy and Ginny stayed for five years. I made a pot of tea every Thursday evening, and we shared our hearts, prayed, and lived life together.

A Mentor Shares—*Sharron*

A young woman I mentored in high school called after returning home from college and wanted to get together and bring a college friend. Thrilled to hear from her, I said yes. Excited to hear how she'd grown in her walk with the Lord, I looked forward to meeting her new friend she valued enough to include in our times together. Throughout the summer, we met weekly at a coffee shop.

Gradually, I discovered a new element in our mentoring relationship: my role had changed. No longer their leader/facilitator, I was a friend who loved God. Through intimate sharing and praying, we grew together in our knowledge of God. I was learning as much from them as they were learning from me—a much older woman.

Years later, I received a text from another young woman. "Free to hang out?" Now in her midthirties, I had mentored the young woman weekly after college, and we'd stayed in contact through emails and texts. I texted back, "Where and when?" As we caught up on our lives, it was as though we never stopped our weekly meetings. Some friendships and mentoring relationships ignore time. I thank God I said yes to his call to be a mentor.

M&M's *from* the Bible Share

Just like Mary, Elizabeth was a woman chosen by God to carry out a divine mission. Luke 1:36 provides the historical landmark of Gabriel telling young Mary she would become miraculously pregnant in the sixth month of her elderly relative Elizabeth's miracle pregnancy. Scripture confirms Elizabeth's child, John the Baptist, would be the forerunner of Mary's child, Jesus Christ, the anticipated Messiah.

Gabriel also was setting the stage for their mentoring relationship: a shared-experience, role-modeling, spiritual-mothering relationship between a much older woman and a young girl transitioning into the season of new wife and mother. Without even sending a message ahead to Elizabeth, Mary shows up at Elizabeth's door and receives a warm greeting from her relative.

Let's Talk about It

1. Why is this season a crossroads in a woman's life?
2. How could this be a difficult season to mentor and receive mentoring?
3. Why don't women see the value of mentoring during this season?
4. How would our culture change if young women had godly mentors?

MARRIAGE SEASON

It is a foolish woman who expects her husband to be to her that which only Jesus Christ Himself can be: ready to forgive, totally understanding, unendingly patient, invariably tender and loving, unfailing in every area, anticipating every need, and making more than adequate provision. Such expectations put a man under an impossible strain. The same goes for the man who expects too much from his wife.

—Ruth Bell Graham[1]

That is why a man leaves his father and mother and is united to his wife, and they become one flesh.

—Genesis 2:24

The marriage season covers a wide spectrum, but the principles of mentoring remain the same because God's Word regarding marriage, communication, finances, and family never changes . . . and God's Word is the foundation for every mentoring relationship. Some women have had the blessing of the same mentor from newlywed years to seasoned married years, and others have found mentors for specific phases of the marriage season. Chapter Twelve discusses parenting, but first comes husband and wife . . . at least in God's original plan. Marriage is an earthly replication of Christ with his church:

> I delight greatly in the LORD;
> my soul rejoices in my God.
> For he has clothed me with garments of salvation
> and arrayed me in a robe of his righteousness,
> as a bridegroom adorns his head like a priest,
> and as a bride adorns herself with her jewels. (Isa. 61:10)

> *As a young man marries a young woman,*
> so will your Builder marry you;
> *as a bridegroom rejoices over his bride,*
> so will your God rejoice over you.
> (Isa. 62:5—emphasis added)

Newlywed to Fifty Years or More

Maybe you looked at this heading and thought, *Needs are different for newlyweds than couples married twenty-five or fifty plus years.* True. The specific details will differ, but the basic truths keeping a marriage on solid ground remain the same, regardless of years together.

I once heard a mentor say her mentee was a newlywed, and since she herself had been married twenty-five years, she expected to be sharing tips about married life with her mentee. But with a wink, she said the mentee taught her a few things about putting a kick back into her own marriage!

Marriage is about giving 100 percent to the one you love unconditionally. The more you give lovingly, not grudgingly, the more you receive back. It never hurts to have a few guidelines you each agree to, but when you reduce the relationship to keeping tallies, it becomes a lose/lose relationship. If both spouses are working, have a conversation regarding a division of chores and household responsibilities—but doing things together is always more fun. Focus on marriage as a team effort and remember that you're on the same team.

Mentor Tips ....

- Never let your time together turn into a gripe session about her husband and marriage. Always bring the conversation back to what she loves about her husband.
- Ask your mentee to introduce you to her husband and explain to him that his wife and you will be spending time in prayer and studying God's Word together.

- Ask your husband what you can share about your own marriage. If he asks you not to share something, then don't. With things he's okay with, use your own life as examples of dealing with marriage issues, and share when something didn't work out well. Let her hear how loving couples arrive at healthy resolutions, even when they don't agree.
- Ask about specific areas where the mentee would like to focus.
- Help her keep realistic expectations about her husband and marriage.
- Do a Bible study on marriage. I particularly like Cynthia Heald's *Loving Your Husband.*
- Help her learn to go to God's Word and prayer when facing challenges, concerns, or worries.
- Listen well, and ask God for discernment and wisdom how to respond.
- Always encourage your mentee to pray for her husband and treat him with respect, like the man she fell in love with, and treat him as the head of their home.
- Unless there are issues of abuse or a potentially dangerous situation, be a cheerleader championing her marriage.
- If there is abuse or criminal behavior in the home, notify your pastor and the authorities and help her find a safe place to stay.

Mentee Tips ....

- Talk with your husband about why you want a mentor. Assure him you won't talk badly about him, and honor your promise. Let him know you would benefit as a wife by talking, praying, and learning from a woman married longer.
- Keep your discussion about yourself and your role in the marriage.

- Let your mentor know specific areas where you struggle and could use prayer, as well as things you enjoy and celebrate.
- Your mentor may see things you don't readily see in yourself. Ask God to help you remain teachable and open to change and growth.
- If your mentor notices areas of abuse, danger, or criminal behavior, she will notify the church and the authorities and help you find a safe place to stay.

God's Perspective: Search the Scriptures Together

- God's plan for unity in marriage—Gen. 1:27–28, 2:21–25; Hosea 2:19
- Marital sex—1 Cor. 7:2–5; Heb. 13:4
- Husband and wife co-partnership—Eph. 5:23, 24, 32; Rom. 12:9–10
- Being a cherished wife—Prov. 12:4, 19:14, 31:10
- A great marriage is between two great forgivers—Eph. 4:32

A Mentee Shares—*Debra Douglas*

Married on Thursday and moved away from home for the first time on Monday, I was thrilled when a sweet lady invited Paul and me for peanut butter sandwiches on our first Sunday in South Carolina. Dot asked if we wanted to listen to a sermon by Major Ian Thomas on tape—a revolutionary idea to me in 1978! The topic—God putting us in a particular place at a particular time for a particular reason—profoundly influenced us. We made the word "put" our family mission statement. God has *put* us in amazing places, beginning with Mrs. Dot's kitchen.

Dot loved God's Word: tears flowed down her "Mrs. Santa Claus" dimpled cheeks as she read Scripture to her young adults Sunday school class. She also understood how to live out Scripture in practical ways. For the next thirty-six years, Dot mentored me according to Titus 2. She poured into my life from her wisdom, life experiences, and biblical knowledge, and confronted me with firmness and love when I drifted away from seeking God's path. When I told her I was going to seminary to pursue a doctoral degree, she cried and begged me to reconsider. Later, she realized God was leading me there and preparing her to help me with the difficult journey.

Dot taught me how to be a wife. She adored her husband without worshipping him. We shared joys, upsets, and great loss. Her own life had been full of challenges, including growing up in an orphanage, battling cancer, sending a son to Vietnam, and losing loved ones. She walked with me through the loss of my mom, encouraged me through infertility treatments, and then enlightened me in raising a wild and active son.

No matter where God *put* us, Dot's mentoring came with us. As the miles increased between us, the distance decreased with Dot's daily devotionals, letters covered with teardrops, earnest phone conversations, and peaceful, restful visits with long, late-night chats. Dot imprinted on my life her passion for Scripture and serving others. I think that's mentoring.

A Mentor Shares—*Joneal Kirby*

Women should have mentors at all stages and ages. I believe we need mentors to encourage us to learn more about ourselves, to explore authentic relationships, and to motivate us to become better at anything we do. Mentors come into our lives to walk us through specific seasons.

When I met Karen, she was an older woman. She and her husband were leaders in almost every category of our church's ministries. Teamwork as a couple was their visible strength, which I admired and respected. So as young newlyweds, it was an honor and a blessing to join these friends regularly for dinners in their home, outings, and game times with other couples. I saw genuine moments of hospitality and began to develop the way I wanted to behave toward folks in my own home.

Karen had a way of gathering different people together. An older widow and a young college student would get to know each other. Younger women, as I was, would become fast friends with an elderly couple seasoned in life experiences. I learned from Karen the deep joy of sharing a meal around a table. Life was an adventure to live with new friends. Karen's influence was more than just in hospitality. She was the first to invite me to teach a Bible study and share my faith in groups.

What I learned from Karen, often in her kitchen, proved to be invaluable for my family life and ministry work, as I went on to lead women's ministries and start Heartfelt Ministries, a Titus 2 women's ministry for women in all ages and seasons of life. Looking back now over forty-one years of marriage, the thousands of people we've shared our home with while sitting around our kitchen table doing Bible studies, or celebrating an occasion, all have the marks of Karen's influence. Those early experiences definitely shaped who I became as a woman, wife, and ministry leader.

A Mentee/Mentor Shares—*Dianne Barker*

During the early years of my marriage, the Lord—knowing I needed a good-wife role model—sent an older woman to mentor me, lovingly teaching me (like the Titus 2:3–5 woman) how to be a wife and homemaker and to make my first priority pleasing the Lord. Later, he sent to my own door young women seeking marriage advice. Over the years dozens came to hear the teaching I'd received, illustrated with stories from my marriage showing how applying God's principles to one's daily walk is the key to a flourishing relationship. Mentoring has been a double blessing—mentored by a precious friend so I could pass on her sound biblical teaching and encourage other young women desiring to strengthen their marriages.

M&M's *from* the Bible Share

I'm sure during the three months Mary spent with Elizabeth and Zacharias, Mary asked Elizabeth many questions about marriage. Mary, betrothed to Joseph, would soon be a wife. Elizabeth, married many years, would have much to tell Mary about keeping house, wifely responsibilities, and the role of the wife in those days (Luke 1:5–56).

Let's Talk about It

1. What are some ways the mentor might help the mentee keep God at the center of her marriage?
2. Sometimes, newlyweds feel an emotional letdown when the excitement of the wedding and honeymoon are over and life gets back to normal. How can the mentor help the mentee maintain marital bliss?
3. How might a newly married mentee encourage a mentor who has been married a number of years?
4. What are the advantages of doing a Bible study or reading a book on marriage together?

Marital Problems

Marriage is between two *imperfect* people who will *always* disappoint and disillusion each other unless they keep *perfect* Jesus at the center of their relationship. That might sound like a bold statement. Certainly many Christian marriages do fail, but that is probably because they didn't keep Jesus at the center of *every* decision, discussion, and disagreement.

Pastor Pete, who married Dave and me, taught a class called Marriage Builders. Each week, he drew a triangle on a white board with God at the pinnacle of the triangle. Then he drew a stick figure man in one bottom corner of the triangle and a stick figure woman at the opposite bottom corner. It was a visual representation that when we try to work through issues on our own, we're the farthest away from each other and God. As each of us individually moves up the triangle toward God, we grow closer to God and to each other.

Many issues subject a couple to divisive onslaughts attacking a marriage: finances, parenting, jealousy, in-laws, personality differences, loneliness, illness, outside attractions, work . . . daily life. Statistics of crumbling marriages—even among Christians—indicate Satan is winning the spiritual battle in many homes because couples haven't armed themselves with the only effective offensive weapon— the sword of the Spirit—the Word of God. How many marriages might elude divorce if spouses had mentors praying for and with them, teaching them how to study their Bibles daily, and showing them how to put God back on the throne in their marriage and family?

In a struggling marriage, it's too easy to focus on what's wrong instead of stopping to seek God's wise counsel and listening to *his* guidance in making things right again.

Mentor Tips ....

Refer back to the Mentor Tips in the Newlywed to Fifty Years or More season of this chapter: those tips still apply, whether the mentee is happily married or struggling. Here are several more suggestions when problems arise:

- Watch the DVD, or stream the movie, *War Room* together, which has mentoring relationships as a central focus and the use of spiritual warfare (Eph. 6:10–18) to combat serious marital problems. In *War Room*, the mentor doesn't dissect the marriage problems, try to change the husband, or devise retaliation schemes. Instead, she teaches the mentee how to fight for her marriage with the sword of the Spirit, the Word of God, and prayer.
- Don't become embroiled in their issues.
- Don't take sides.
- Help the mentee work on her own issues, not her husband's.
- Pray Scripture together to stay focused on God's will, not the mentee's desire to have things her way. Teach her how to pray Scripture and journal. (See the Appendix.)
- If the issue is abuse or potential harm to the mentee and family, she may need to remove herself from the situation. Ask your pastor to intervene or help her notify the authorities.

Mentee Tips ....

- Refer to the Mentee Tips in the Newlywed to Fifty Years or More season of the chapter, because you want your marriage to last fifty years or longer.
- You may be hurt, mad, angry, sad, disappointed, guilty, or frustrated. Those are natural feelings, but what you do with those feelings can harm or help your marriage. Let your mentor help you work through negative emotions. You can't change your husband, but you can change how you respond to him and to the issues.

- Watch the movie *War Room* with an open mind that God can, and will, restore your marriage if you let him.
- Be honest with your mentor, and yourself, regarding *your* role in the problems.
- Your mentor can't fix your marriage or take sides, but she can pray with you and help you work through your emotions and options.
- If you experience an abusive or threatening situation, tell your mentor and let her talk with a pastor to find a safe place for you to go or let her help you notify authorities.

God's Perspective: Search the Scriptures Together

Most of the issues causing marital problems revolve around the following areas:

- Selfishness—Matt. 22:36–40; Rom. 12:3
- Pride—Ps. 25:9; James 4:10
- Rights—1 Cor. 7:4, 8:9
- Your fight isn't against your husband (spiritual warfare)— Eph. 6:10–18; James 4:7
- When the husband isn't a believer, the wife can be an example of godliness to her spouse—1 Cor. 7:13–15
- A key component of marriage is being two good forgivers— Matt. 6:15, 18:21–22; Phil. 2:5–8

A Mentee Shares—*Jocelyn Green*

Military life is hard on marriages, and many don't survive the separations, re-entries after deployment, and loneliness. They encounter numerous issues that would test any marriage, which is why looking at how military wives survive marital difficulties helps *all* marriages. The wife may be a mature Christian, but she's in a new challenging season.

Two days after marrying my Coast Guard officer husband, we moved from Washington, D.C., to his next duty station in Homer, Alaska. I was alone for seven months of our first year of marriage, unemployed, and nearly friendless. I attended two Bible studies, joined book clubs, volunteered at the nursing home, and drove a woman with cancer to medical appointments five hours away. But the most meaningful times were with another Coast Guard wife who took me into her home and gave me coffee, conversation, and a healthy dose of perspective.

I didn't view our friendship as a mentoring relationship at the time, but it was. She had years of experience as a Coast Guard wife and was a beacon of joy and peace. Several other wives my age were bitter, gossipy, and toxic. My mentor-friend modeled the single most important lesson: focus on God's character, not on our circumstances. This woman walked beside me in gentle but important ways. Without her, I may have slipped into the unhealthy habit of bemoaning my hardships instead of cultivating a grateful heart for blessings I already had.

A Mentor Shares—*Joyce*

We've been married for thirty-seven years, and for twenty-six of those we moved wherever the military sent us—seventeen moves. Each new location meant making new friends. When I was the new military wife in Germany, Franka and I walked to a playground where the kids played while we talked. A pastor's wife, Franka mentored me in adjusting to military life and my husband being gone 30, 60, or 90 days on training exercises.

Another mentor, Caroline, taught me how to be a military wife—what to wear and how to get through a temporary duty assignment. She listened as I started raising my babies and prayed for me for over twenty years, until we left the military.

I passed on what Franka and Caroline taught me by mentoring other military wives—some younger, and others in my season of life. When I was homeschooling, mentee Kimmi didn't have children yet, but she sought me out after taking a class on spiritual mothering. We cross-stitched and talked while I baked bread and brownies.

I met Chris when our sons were in high school. Chris was a new believer, and we did a Bible study at her house while her kids played. When Chris later became the president of a large ministry for women, a position I previously held, God called upon me to mentor her. I phoned weekly to give support and guidance.

Amanda and Sarah wanted to run with me and asked continual questions about military life. When our sons were in college and our husbands deployed in Iraq, Debbi and I read a book and then discussed it, as we decorated her bedroom to surprise her husband when he returned home.

Martie and I were involved in ministry at our military chapel. One morning a week we walked. Heading out, we shared prayer requests; returning, we took turns praying for each other.

Connie was a few years older, and her husband was more senior in military rank than my husband. She helped better my golf game while we talked about military life and our adult children.

M&M's *from* the Bible Share

Priscilla and Aquila weathered many changes in their married life, but they worked and served together as a team. Tentmakers with the apostle Paul, they repeatedly picked up their business and home to follow Paul as missionaries. Moving and re-establishing their business had to cause some strife and short tempers, but we never read about marital problems. Instead, as they moved from place to place, they held church in their home and mentored Apollos, who needed to know the whole gospel so he could preach and teach effectively (Acts 18:26). Priscilla and Aquila managed the fine art of balancing work, ministry, and marriage.

Let's Talk about It

1. What issues typically cause marital problems?
2. How have you seen God help you work through a problem in your marriage?
3. Describe a time when you didn't seek God's guidance during marital strife.
4. Why do you think so many couples give up on their marriages today?

CHAPTER ELEVEN

SINGLE OR SPIRITUALLY SINGLE SEASON

Our mentoring group supported one of my engaged mentees when the engagement broke up. Mentors walk alongside; they comfort and guide, and keep pointing them to Jesus.

　—Bobette

Learn to do right; seek justice.
Defend the oppressed.
Take up the cause of the fatherless;
plead the case of the widow.

　—Isaiah 1:17

A woman at any age can find herself in the single season, maybe not by choice:

- Never married and still hoping to meet "Mr. Right"; many singles are anxious to find a man to marry—especially if their biological clock is ticking
- Divorced—either by choice or not—and grieving the loss of the dream of living happily ever after, or not being part of a couple
- Widowed and grieving the traumatic loss of a mate and life partner
- Spiritually single—married to an unbeliever

If you're unhappily single, please seek out a mentor to listen, pray, encourage, and help discover God's plan for your life in this season. Mr. Right is a myth created by romantic novelists and movies. Often, divorce documents cite "irreconcilable differences," but going into marriage expecting to agree on everything forever is foolish and fantasy. Marriage is between an imperfect man and imperfect woman with different pasts, thoughts, ideas, and personalities united in an imperfect relationship. We don't *find* a soulmate. We *become* soulmates when we find someone willing to let Jesus help us work through all the differences and imperfections, and keep him at the center of the relationship. In the process, *Jesus Christ* binds our souls together.

If you are happily single and enjoying your independence, and God is helping you accept and embrace this single season, awesome. Share how you found this peace with a mentee, and tell her what helps you stay strong and hopeful as a single.

In a world with few moral boundaries, dating has challenges. A man calling himself a "Christian" may not necessarily be a godly man you'd want to date. Sadly, not all Christians stay sexually pure or adhere to living a godly moral life. If you're divorced or a widow, you might entertain the thought that since you're not a virgin anymore, it wouldn't hurt to add sex to the relationship. You need a Bible-believing Christian mentor to guide you to God's Word on sexual morality and help you prayerfully wait for the godly man you deserve. Don't settle for less than God's best.

Maybe you're what I call spiritually single—you are a believer who married an unbeliever, or he walked away from God and no longer professes faith, or you became a Christian after you married an unbeliever. It's difficult to stay strong in your faith when your marriage partner doesn't share your beliefs and values. You can learn a great deal from women who love their husbands well but love God more.

If widowed, divorced, or unhappily never married, grieving is a season you shouldn't endure alone. At first, you may want to be alone, but crying, praying, venting, and connecting with another woman who understands your heartache—and who can give you a hug when you're down—will help you through the dark times of discouragement, loss, and possible depression.

Mentor Tips ....

Whether you're married now or single (for the same reason as your mentee, or a different reason), help her through the emotional, physical, and spiritual challenges—or rollercoaster—she's facing.

- If your mentee is newly divorced, see if there's a divorce-care group at a church in her area. Remind her that she's still vulnerable and that the purpose of this group is *not* dating, but to learn the steps to moving on after divorce.
- If your mentee is a new widow, find a grief support group to help supplement your mentoring times together.
- If your mentee is never married, and wants to be, gently help her discover any changes she might need to make in dating, or personally, and suggest places to meet the kind of man she deserves.
- If your mentee is married to an unbeliever, help her show grace and the irresistible love of Christ to her husband. Remind her she's the closest to Jesus her husband will ever get. Pray with her for his salvation. Watch the movie *The Case for Christ* together—a true story of a wife who becomes a Christian after marriage and then unconditionally loves and prays for her atheist husband during his search for Christ.
- Do a Bible study focusing on being the bride of Christ.

Mentee Tips ....

Your mentor isn't a counselor, psychologist, or matchmaker; but she can help you through this season by reminding you of the Great Counselor and Heavenly Husband, who *does* have all the answers and solutions to life's challenges. God will help you find a way to add purpose to this season.

God's Perspective: Search the Scriptures Together

- Grief and despair—Ps. 30:10–12; Isa. 61:1–3; Jer. 31:13; Rev. 21:4
- A season of waiting for a believing spouse—Ps. 27:14, 33:20; 2 Cor. 6:14
- Maintaining hope—Ps. 25:5, 25:21, 31:24, 42:5
- If tempted to become sexually active, God says flee from sexual sin—1 Cor. 6:12–14, 6:18; 1 Thess. 4:2–6
- Married to an unbeliever—1 Cor. 7:13–17
- We are the brides of Christ—Rev. 19:7

A Mentee Shares—*Rosalie*

When I met Linda, she had started the Woman to Woman Mentoring Ministry at my church. We became fast friends and promoted the mentoring ministry together. Eight years later, my husband died. A few weeks after his passing, this dear lady invited me to a luncheon at her home on Memorial Day. Linda had become a widow a few years prior and knew the pain and grief of losing a spouse. She said holidays are the hardest because when family and friends celebrate as couples, they rarely include widows in their activities.

Linda decided to remedy this heartache by reaching out to women going through grief and loss and started her own ministry, Celebration of Life. Her friendship and compassion helped through those difficult first months as a widow. She was a mentor who cared, and I thank God for her comfort. I have a peace and contentment from relying on the Lord more and more. Even though I'm living alone, God is present and helps me through everything I face.

A Mentor Shares—*Bobette*

My young, single women friends are the ones I mentored most. We met weekly at my home for a Bible study. I prayed for each one and regularly had supper for them, where we talked about what was happening in their lives. I tried to gently guide and point them to Jesus. Some of it took; some of it didn't.

A Mentor Shares—*Esther*

One wintery Sunday morning the snow was so deep that no churches in our community met. A retired pastor lives two doors up from us, so I called and asked if we could do church together. He suggested inviting our neighbor Janie, recently divorced after thirty-five years of marriage, and her son. We had "church," and Janie shared some of her needs. I felt the Lord wanted me to ask Janie if she would like me to mentor her, and she happily said yes. It's easy to make excuses when just two of you meet, but we finally made it through *Life on the Highest Plane* before she sold her house and moved away. I saw God working in her life and tried to encourage her in difficult changes. He knows the end.

M&M's *from* the Bible Share

In the story of Naomi and Ruth (in the Book of Ruth), both women were widows when they went back to Bethlehem together. Naomi, the spiritually older mother-in-law, had much to teach the new believer Ruth about her new faith and the customs of Naomi's homeland. Naomi taught Ruth how to glean the fields for food, and Ruth provided their sustenance. Two single widows looking out for each other. One of the customs was for a Kinsmen Redeemer to maintain the lineage of Naomi's husband, so Naomi actually helped her daughter-in-law find a new husband, Boaz.

Initially, these two single women's lives looked desolate and lonely. As they stayed true to each other and the Lord, God rewarded Ruth with a husband and baby, and Naomi with a grandson in the lineage of Jesus. While Naomi was bitter at first (Ruth 1:13, 20), she rallied when she had a mentee who needed her to set a good example and be a role model. Mentoring is always a two-way relationship.

Let's Talk about It

1. What are some of the biggest challenges of this season?
2. How can you find contentment?
3. Where are some healthy places to find godly companionship?
4. What boundaries should you set for dating when, and if, you're ready?

CHAPTER TWELVE

PARENTING SEASON

Looking back on my life, I have found one of the most helpful ways to gain perspective on your current situation is to see parenthood in terms of seasons. There is the season of starting a family and the ensuing baby/toddler years, the season of raising teens, the season of the empty nest, and, for some, the "bungee cord" season—when you thought your nest was empty and a child comes home again. Then there's the season of the golden years.

—Susan Yates[1]

Parenting is near and dear to my heart. I consider it a pleasure to lend support and what-worked and what-didn't-work to younger moms. Oh my, where has the time gone? When did I become one of the older moms?

—Julie

*Children's children are a crown to the aged,
and parents are the pride of their children.*

—Proverbs 17:6

Parenting has a vast array of subseasons and life experiences, so I grouped together those with crossover mentoring principles. But you'll want to check some of the other subseasons for ideas also. Every mom wants to talk to another mom who has survived each new phase of mothering and parenting.

Pregnancy—Planned and Unplanned

Pregnancy is typically a joyful season for women who are ready and excited to have a child. But if the pregnancy is unplanned—maybe unwanted or unexpected—there may be no joy or excitement. Either way, it's crucial to have a mentor during this time of extensive body and hormonal changes. But unfortunately, many women go through these nine months, or early pregnancy decisions, without another woman to talk to and ask questions.

- If this is your first pregnancy, find a woman you admire who has kids and ask her to mentor you.
- If this is an unplanned pregnancy, quickly find a spiritual mentor who can give you encouragement, support, and help you locate a Christian crisis-pregnancy center. Only listen to advice from a biblical perspective with options that protect the life of your unborn baby. If you cannot find a mentor right away, a crisis pregnancy center will have counselors available to help you and offer encouragement and support.
- If you learn of a woman who is newly pregnant, and you've been pregnant, offer to mentor her.

Mentor Tips ....

- *Planned Pregnancy*—If she has questions, share whatever helped you through morning sickness, body changes, stretch marks, diet, cravings, preparing a nursery, delivery, breast-feeding decisions, and bringing the precious baby home. New information and products are available continuously, so have fun researching together, but always refer to her doctor for any medical questions. Be mindful of not scaring her or telling horror stories of difficult pregnancies and deliveries, even if those were your experiences. Share in her joy and enthusiasm and help alleviate any fears or apprehension.
- *Unplanned Pregnancy*—This could be an inconvenient pregnancy or one the mentee doesn't want to continue—either can occur even in marriages. If it is an inconvenient pregnancy that she has chosen to continue, she needs lots of

encouragement, support, and prayer. If she is considering terminating, in addition to the information here, go to the Teen Mom season of this chapter (even if she's not a teen) for suggestions on life-giving options and scriptural passages to guide you in mentoring her to not abort her baby, but give the baby life. It will also be helpful to read about the trauma women suffer after abortion discussed in Chapter Thirteen, Post-Abortion, to help your mentee understand the long-term effects mentally, emotionally, and spiritually. Share with her Pastor Rick Warren's truth: "There are accidental parents, but there are no accidental children."

Mentee Tips

This is a personal and usually joyous time—a tiny baby full of new life is growing in your womb! Or it could be a time of confusion, fear, and uncertainty.

- If this is your first pregnancy, ask your mentor questions as they arise. Giving birth to a baby is an event only another woman who has experienced pregnancy can truly appreciate and understand. There are no "silly" questions, so ask them all!
- If this is not your first pregnancy, and you have other children, let your mentor provide ideas and suggestions of how she balanced childrearing and pregnancy.
- If this is not a joyous time, let your mentor help you make the necessary adjustments and choices to protect your baby. Share with her your honest concerns, and keep an open mind to the suggestions and options she offers. God never makes a mistake, and he has a plan and a purpose for your baby.

God's Perspective: Search the Scriptures Together

For additional scriptural readings on the value of a baby's life in God's eyes, go to the God's Perspective: Search the Scriptures Together section in the Teen Mom season of this chapter.

- Pregnancy is a time to praise the Lord for new life—Ps. 8:1–4
- God has a plan for every child—Ps. 127:3; Eccles. 11:5; Jer. 1:5
- When you make the right decision for your unborn baby, God will take care of you and the child—Isa. 59:1

A Mentee Shares—*Alicia*

My mentor, Debbie, didn't realize she's been mentoring me since she helped me through my unplanned pregnancy and the birth of my baby girl years ago. She thought she was just being a friend, but it was so much more. She's still a big part of our life.

A Mentor Shares—*Debbie (Alicia's mentor)*

As a newlywed, I started a new job, where I met Alicia. We began walking together at lunchtime and talking about life. Alicia was single, and one day she said she was pregnant and unsure of what would happen next. She needed to leave where she was living, so my husband and I moved her in with us. I asked our friend Richard from church to help with the move. Thus began Alicia's relationship with her now husband.

My husband and I talked with Alicia about the Bible and life's problems and invited her to our church, which, to her amazement, gave her a baby shower.

The first time we had Richard over to our home, Alicia's water broke. The four of us were in the labor room when her daughter made a fast escape. The next eight

months flew by with Alicia and Richard's dating, engagement, and wedding, and Alicia becoming a Christian. Our
relationship changed but was no less fun, and mentoring
continued. We talked about everything, including the Bible.

Mentoring can start by first helping with physical
needs, and then moving into spiritual mentoring. I don't
know why God thought newlyweds should have a pregnant
girl living with us. I would advise my kids against it, but it
came naturally. I had the blessing of growing up to believe
in God's divine intervention, and God wanted us to help
Alicia and her unborn baby.

Thirty years later, Alicia feels I've mentored her. I'm a
little older, but I thought we mentored each other. We talk
nearly every day and spend many holidays together as families. Alicia and I have been through parents dying, children's problems, marriage trials, financial issues, spiritual
challenges, and watching our older four kids grow up
together and move out on their own. And through all the
seasons . . . we talk about the Bible.

M&M's *from* the Bible Share

Leah, one of Jacob's wives, had seven children. She embraced each
new baby—six sons and one daughter—with names reflecting her joy
in being a mother. Leah never felt truly loved by Jacob and felt over-
shadowed by her younger sister Rachel—not a good reason for having
children. Still, she was a good mother to *all* her children, rejoiced
in each pregnancy, and was a faithful wife (Gen. 29:31–35, 30:17–21).

Let's Talk about It

1. What are some highs and lows of pregnancy?
2. How are children a gift from God?

3. Debbie in the A Mentor Shares section mentioned divine intervention. Have you had examples in your life?
4. Debbie readily helped Alicia. Have you been in a similar situation and helped someone in need?

Teen Mom

Chapter Eight discussed the unquestionable value of mentoring tween and teen girls to live pure and godly lives during these formative years. But unfortunately, they don't always follow a mentor's or parent's wise advice and counsel. Many young girls succumb to peer pressure and become sexually active, ending up pregnant and terrified. While looking for statistics on teen pregnancy, I came across a site with these alarming facts:

- Three in ten teen American girls will get pregnant *at least once* before age twenty. That's nearly 750,000 teen pregnancies every year.
- Parenthood is the leading reason that teen girls drop out of school. More than 50 percent of teen mothers never graduate from high school.
- About 25 percent of teen moms have a second child within twenty-four months of having their first baby.
- Fewer than 2 percent of teen moms earn a college degree by age thirty.
- The United States has one of the highest teen pregnancy rates in the western industrialized world.
- Almost 50 percent of teens have never considered how a pregnancy would affect their lives.[2]

The good news of these statistics is that many of these young girls choose to have their babies rather than abort them. If you're a teen mom, a mentor can offer support, encouragement, and spiritual mentoring during the pregnancy and help you with the decisions you make for your baby's future.

Mentor Tips ....

What do you do when your teen mentee says she's pregnant? You may be the only one she feels safe telling. As in all mentoring scenarios, pray with her for wisdom and guidance from the Lord. She needs to tell her parents and may ask you to accompany her. As discussed in Chapter Eight, if she's a teen still at home, her parents should know you're mentoring her from a Christian perspective. Her pregnancy will be a huge shock, as it probably was for you to hear from someone you hoped was following your godly counsel.

Keep the pregnancy all about her and not about you. Every mentee is responsible for her choices and consequences. Now she has another human being to consider—her unborn baby.

Her parents may want her to put the baby up for adoption. The birth mother of my precious adopted grandson was fifteen years old, and he was her second baby. The teen's mother insisted she put him up for adoption at birth. That brave decision blessed our family, but I often wonder if this young girl received any mentoring or counseling to overcome the grief of giving up her baby and to prevent her getting pregnant again.

Maybe your mentee's family is considering abortion rather than adoption. You, as the spiritual mentor, can play a significant role in helping the family, and the teen, understand the lingering consequences of this action, and pray with them to choose life for this precious unborn baby. Read the Post-Abortion Recovery season of Chapter Thirteen for help in discussing the lingering psychological, physical, and spiritual repercussions of abortion.

Pray your mentee and her parents choose to give her baby life, which will entail more decisions. Ask her parents if you can continue mentoring her, and maybe mentor Mom too. If your mentee chooses to raise her baby as a teen mom, depending on the support she gets at home, she needs someone to answer her many questions, give practical advice, and provide encouragement in this new season.

If her parents aren't agreeable to her having the baby and cast her out of the home, or she's already out of the house and on her own, help her find a Christian organization providing homes for teen moms and ask at your church. As her mentor, your role isn't to provide for her, but many places are equipped to help her.

If the choice is to give up the baby for adoption, you can guide her (and the family) through the process of finding a Christian adoption agency. While she may feel initial relief, she always will be a birth mom, so look for signs of depression, sadness, grief, and acting out.

Mentee Tips ....

I know this isn't how you expected to enter motherhood, but you made a godly choice to give your baby life and a brave decision to raise your baby . . . but you need help. Check in your area for Christian mentoring organizations for teen moms. You can find one by googling and asking at your church. In most states, if you're under eighteen, your parents will have the final say in the choices you make, and your mentor can help you adjust to those decisions. Don't pit your mentor against your parents, but do ask your parents to include your mentor in the discussions.

God's Perspective: Search the Scriptures Together

Following are scriptural passages to share with your mentee and her family, to show God is pro-life. Also look at the suggested scriptural readings in the Pregnancy—Planned and Unplanned season of this chapter, page 135.

- God personally created *each* embryo and has a plan for *every* unborn life—Job 10:8–12, 12:10; Ps. 139:13, 16; Isa. 44:2; Gal. 1:15

- God says to protect innocent life—Exod. 20:13; Jer. 7:6
- God wants us to choose life—Deut. 30:19

A Mentee Shares—*Stephanie Shott*

I caught a glimpse of her as she walked across the parking lot. She looked about sixteen. Young in years, great with child. Reflecting on my teen pregnancy, I couldn't help but wonder if she was ready for the journey ahead. Did she grasp the greatness of her newfound role and how everything she had ever known was about to change? Would someone walk with her through motherhood or would she have to go it alone?

I was eighteen when my son was born and had no idea what it meant to be a mom. I thought the whole thing would be a breeze, but my dream of motherhood was so different from reality. I was a single mom, without Christ, without a mentor, and without a clue.

As the years passed, I married and became a Christian. Everything changed, except I still didn't have a mentor, and I still barely had a clue.

That was twenty-seven years ago, and as I reflect on the way I muddled through motherhood, I wonder: Where are all the mentors? I remember looking up to several women in the church, but I was never able to wiggle my way under their wing. It shouldn't have been so hard, and no mom should have to go it alone. The church should weave mentoring into the fabric of the church. Right?

A Mentor Shares—*Genny Heikka*

About six months after Katie [my daughter] was born, I heard a guest speaker at church talk about the need in my community for mentors for teen moms. I instantly felt a tug on my heart. Being a new mom myself, I knew how challenging taking care of a baby could be. I tried to imagine what it would be like to be a teenager with a newborn, and it choked me up. I couldn't deny the pull I felt to get involved.

But, quickly, doubt set in . . .

Me? I thought. A mentor to teen moms? Who am I to help other moms when I'm just learning how to be a mom myself?

I brought home a brochure that the guest speaker had handed out and read more about the Mentor Mom program through Youth for Christ. But I didn't call. Instead, I listened to that voice of doubt that said I wasn't good enough, or ready enough . . . and I talked myself out of responding. . . .

But even though I didn't take action right away, the pull I felt wouldn't leave. I remember looking at Katie asleep in her bassinet and marveling at her—her tiny hands, her rosy cheeks, her little feet. And then I would think about the teen moms who might be looking at their babies too, and I wondered how they felt about being a mom.

When Mike [my husband] was out of town (he travelled a lot during that time), and I would be up in the middle of the night with Katie crying, I sometimes felt alone and exhausted. And I would think about how alone those teen moms might be feeling.

I was confused by the pull I felt to get involved and help. It didn't make sense to me—this tug to mentor young moms. I felt totally inadequate, and truthfully, the thought of being a mentor scared me. . . .

Against all logic, and unsure how it would turn out, I finally ended up pushing aside the doubt and I called the

Mentor Mom program, went through their training, and got involved in their mentor program. I was scared and unsure, but God knew more than I did that He had given me a passion to encourage other moms. A passion and strength I didn't even know I had yet.

Over the next several years in that program, I had the privilege of coming alongside teen moms—moms with different stories, different backgrounds, and different challenges—and mentoring them. I didn't have parenting all figured out (I still don't!), and I didn't have a lot of experience.

But I quickly learned that wasn't what it was all about. It was about saying yes and using my gifts to be there for a teen mom during a hard time . . . letting her know she wasn't alone in her frustrations and questions . . . supporting her as she learned, and . . . helping her understand how much God loves her.

Sometimes, I think we don't fully discover our strengths because we let doubt or fear keep us from moving forward. When we feel a tug on our hearts . . . it is there for a reason. Yet so often, we minimize these feelings, put things off for later, or hold back because we doubt our feelings or our own abilities. When we do that, we miss an opportunity to make a difference. We miss a chance to see how God can take that small seed of desire (that He planted in our hearts to begin with) and grow it. But when we say yes—even if we aren't sure if we're qualified or how it's all going to turn out—that's when He opens new doors to discover, live, and love our strengths . . . that's when lives are changed, including ours . . . one by one, the world is changed too.[3]

M&M's *from* the Bible—Elizabeth and Mary

At Christmas, we read in Luke 1:26–56 the story of the angel Gabriel's visit with teenage Mary, where he reveals she will become the mother of the Messiah. Previously, in Luke 1:5–25, another miracle revelation came to Mary's elderly, infertile relative Elizabeth: she would have a baby, because "nothing is impossible with God!"

Luke 1:39 says, "Mary got ready and hurried" to the hill country, over 50 miles away, to visit Elizabeth, who was then six months pregnant. Elizabeth welcomed her teenage, unmarried, pregnant relative: she wasn't repulsed or condescending (Luke 1:40–45). Mentor Elizabeth surely shared with mentee Mary how to face people's stares and disapproval, while also offering pregnancy, marriage, and housekeeping tips.

Let's Talk about It

1. Were you a teen mom? If so, did anyone mentor or help you?
2. What if a "Genny" had mentored Stephanie when she was a clueless, lonely teen mom?
3. How could you support and encourage a teen mom?
4. What would be your reaction if a Stephanie (or a Mary) showed up on your doorstep?

New Mom

Every mom remembers the shocking reality of being a new mom for the first time—the lack of sleep and personal time . . . what to do about diaper rash . . . is this *normal* for a baby? Today's moms often go to the Internet for answers, but nothing replaces the assurance and comfort of a live person to commiserate with and maybe even shed a few exhausted tears with.

I remember saying, "When does a new mom have time to take a shower or eat?" First-time motherhood can be overwhelming and sometimes lonely, as you feel isolated from the outside world. As much as you love your new baby, communication reduces to cries, screams, gurgles, and giggles. Hormonal changes throw some women into a desperate time of depression. Or there's a panic attack when your mom, or mother-in-law, eventually must go home. My daughter cried as she watched me drive down the street after being with her for a month when her second baby was born only nine months after adopting her infant son. It was like having twins! She did great, but there was the initial feeling of "How am I going to do this by myself?"

Julie's mentor, just a little ahead of her in new motherhood, helped her get a one-year-old baby on a routine: "She taught me how to bring order to our household. Shared books she gleaned from and walked me through getting him to sleep through the night, teething, nursing. . . . Invaluable advice saved my sanity, which I've shared with many new moms over the years."

Mentor Tips ....

Beware of creating an expectation of becoming a surrogate grand-mother, mother, or auntie. However, as a seasoned mom, you know the kind of moral support and encouragement your new-mommy mentee needs right now. It might be difficult for her to get out to a Bible study, so use your time together to pray and dig into God's Word. Offer to meet at her home while the baby sleeps or at night when her husband can watch the baby. Answer "new mom" questions, but be sure she leaves your times together spiritually refilled and refreshed.

Mentee Tips ....

Being a new mom is overwhelming at times, and your mentor might seem like an anchor in the storm, but don't cling to her as a life pre-server. Let her lead you to the Creator of Life and Preserver of Sanity. Ask her all your "new mommy" questions, but also allow time to pray and grow spiritually. Time spent with the Father makes you a better mom and wife.

Your mentor made it through this time, as did many other new moms, and you will too. Let her help you enjoy a season none of us ever gets to relive—the first few weeks and months with your precious gift from God.

God's Perspective: Search the Scriptures Together

- God wants you to have times of rest, even as a new mom— Ps. 16:8–10, 46:10a, 62:1
- Let overjoyed replace overwhelmed—Ps. 5:11, 16:11
- God provides all you need in this, and every, season— Exod. 15:2; Ps. 22:19, 28:7

A Mentee Shares—*Jamie*

Married only a few years, we were in a season of newness: new city, new ministry, new mom with a four-month-old. I longed for a friend and mentor. I had so many questions about being a new mother and the wife of a husband in ministry. I felt lonely and cried out to God about my struggles. Then I heard about the Woman to Woman Mentoring Ministry at our church and knew I should participate.

I met Sheri at the introductory coffee, and we hit it off. It was no surprise when the prayer team matched Sheri as my mentor. We began meeting regularly, and Sheri spoke the truth God wanted me to hear. She blessed my life and was a huge spiritual growth catalyst.

One Sunday morning when my husband was out of town on business and I was pregnant with our second child, I saw what every pregnant woman dreads: bleeding. I cried out to the Lord, "Who can I call?" *Sheri, call Sheri.*

I called my mentor and dear friend. As I choked out the words, she said, "My husband and I will be there soon. We'll take you to the hospital, and my girls will watch your son." Sheri didn't just speak things of the Lord; she (and her whole family) walked through life with my family and me. I was in a crisis, and Sheri was there for me. I was so grateful to the Lord for giving me such a wonderful friend and mentor.

The crisis passed and, a few months later, I gave birth to a healthy son. Sheri and her family were there to rejoice with us. Our mentor/mentee relationship was so much more than a Bible study together. We invested in each other's lives and were stronger together. Our bond will last for eternity because we're sisters in the Lord.

Sheri and I live in different states now, but we talk often. I love hearing Sheri's, "Hey girlfriend!" When we talk, it's as if time hasn't passed.

A Mentor Shares—*Katie and Ellie (Co-mentors)*

Sometimes M&M's share the mentor role as "co-mentors," and mentor each other.

Life changed dramatically when I married and had a child and was no longer part of the singles group, attending events with my singles "family." I especially felt growing pains as a new mother.

One Sunday at Saddleback Church, there was an announcement about a Woman to Woman Mentoring Orientation Coffee to learn about mentoring and becoming either a mentor or mentee. I attended the Orientation Coffee and enjoyed myself immensely.

I was matched with my mentor, Ellie. She had two girls, ages two and five, and my daughter was three years old. We had a lot to share! Although I was officially the mentee, we decided early on we would be "co-mentors," and share and encourage each other in this new-mom season of life.

Over the years, we each moved to different states, but when I speak with Ellie, a trial turns into a lesson. Our girls are now in college, and God has used Ellie on numerous occasions to help me see a situation from God's perspective. She sends CDs on parenting and inspirational books to help shape my life. The mentoring coffee turned into a gift that will last a lifetime. I'm so grateful God put it on the heart of one woman to take action on a ministry idea—Ellie and I are forever changed.

M&M's *from* the Bible Share

Commentators speculate that since Elizabeth was in her sixth month of pregnancy when Mary came to visit, and Mary stayed for three months, she probably helped Elizabeth give birth to John the Baptist (Luke 1:36–56). Mary would observe first-time mom Elizabeth taking care of a newborn. I'm sure Mary was of great assistance to Elizabeth during this transition season, and learned much to apply to giving birth to her own son in a manger under less-than-ideal conditions. These new mothers had to rely heavily on the Lord.

Let's Talk about It

1. Why is *time* sometimes the best gift you can give a new mom?
2. What were the biggest surprises you had as a new mom?
3. What were some first-time mom blessings?
4. How does knowing your baby is acting *normal* help alleviate anxiety?

Mothering

Every mother needs a mentor—find one who has successfully weathered the specific challenges of your current mothering season, then you reciprocate and mentor a mom going through the season you just survived. Those further along in the mothering season must be ready to mentor moms in the throes of raising godly kids. And the only way to raise godly kids is to be godly moms. Remember, your kids are watching, listening, and questioning your every move and word, so let your actions and speech match what you preach and teach.

Mentor Tips ....

- Listen carefully before making suggestions.
- Every family is different.
- Build your mentee up; don't tear her down.
- She may become defensive and not receive advice in the manner you intend if you don't praise her for loving her children enough to seek wise counsel.
- Make praise sincere and not a lead-in to harsh, judgmental criticism.
- Ask questions and offer ideas, but remain humble; don't be prideful, as if you have all the answers and why hasn't she figured this out yet. Try something like, "Wow, I remember that those preschool (or whatever) years are really tough. What helped me survive was. . . ." You identify with her struggle and kindly offer suggestions, instead of telling her what to do.
- Look for the "aha" moments in her posture and responses to confirm she's resonating with you. If you don't see confirmation, return to asking questions, listening, and responding with sensitivity to her issues. Annetta says, "No one helped me understand that much of what I encountered in the teen

mothering season were normal things all kids go through . . . and mothers hurt and cry."

Mentee Tips ....

You chose a mentor you admire for her parenting skills, so don't become defensive when she offers suggestions. She's not trying to make you feel inadequate or incompetent. She wants to provide some tried-and-tested relief-giving mothering techniques. Gratefully receive what might work for your family, and mentally file others for future reference.

God's Perspective: Search the Scriptures Together

To know God's plan for raising children, we need to know our Bibles and know his Word. If we want to use Scripture to discipline and guide our children and teach them how to use it in their lives, we need to know Scripture and use it ourselves.

- Read your Bible daily—Deut. 6:6–9; Ps. 34:11
- Discipline is part of God's plan for raising children, who are all born knowing how to do wrong; it's the parents' job to guide them in the path to righteous living—Job 5:17; Ps. 51:5; Prov. 12:1, 13:24, 19:18, 29:17; Heb. 12:11
- Our role as mothers is to raise our children to be progressively independent of us and persistently dependent on the Lord, his ways, and his words—Prov. 22:6
- A prayerless parent is a powerless parent—1 Thess. 5:17

A Mentee Shares—*Julie*

Sherry has been my "go-to" woman since the day we met. Sherry and her husband trained in Growing Kids God's Way, and my hub and I were intrigued. When my oldest son was one and a half and I was pregnant with our younger son, we took a parenting class at their house.

Sherry became the one I called when my toddler was going through this-or-that stage, we were struggling with potty training, I felt spiritually dry, or I just wanted someone to talk to older than single digits.

Our relationship morphed over time. She started asking *me* for marriage and communication advice. I'm younger, so this shocked me. Our husbands became good friends too, and the four of us started sharing worship and fellowship through a home Bible study.

Sherry and I continue to walk side by side, even though miles apart. Now our relationship is iron sharpening iron, as our children go through the teen years and on into college. We've covered each other in prayer and showered each other with Scripture. Of course, the Lord is my rock and source of strength and wisdom, but of all my friends, Sherry is the *key* person who shaped and molded me as a wife and mother. I hope someday I influence a life as she influenced mine.

A Mentor Shares—*Melinda Means*

As a young mom, I *so* badly needed a more seasoned mom to help guide me away from foolish choices and selfish attitudes. But the sweet, gray-haired, wise mentor I dreamed of—the one to spend structured time with me weekly—never materialized. Instead, God sent my loving pastor's wife, just a few years older than me, who modeled how to put family before myself in healthy ways. "My kids always know I mean what I say. They never doubt I'm going to follow through," she told me. "Yours have to know that too."

Next, God sent a lifelong friend, a year younger than me, who gave tough love during a difficult time. God used her to strengthen my resolve and muster the courage to make hard choices during a painful season with one of my children. Other mentors gave just what I needed at a crucial season, as I simply observed and learned.

It took years to recognize *these* were my Titus 2 women. My mentor just didn't arrive in the package I expected. My Titus 2 woman could look *just like me*. Many moms do have wise older women who pour into their lives regularly. Today, I count myself among them. But as a young mom, I found the search for traditional mentoring difficult. I discovered mentors have no age requirement. They just must be humble, godly, honest, and willing to share the wisdom of their life experiences. As moms, we can learn a lot from women a stage or two ahead of us in the parenting journey. I had to look beyond my idea of what a mentor *should* look like and ask myself some questions:

- Do I have a friend highly skilled in an area of mothering where I struggle?
- What woman do I admire for her godly character?
- Have I observed someone who handles difficult situations with her husband, children, or life in a way I respect and want to emulate?

All it takes to benefit from the wisdom and experience of one of these women is a teachable heart, keen observation, and the humility to ask for help and guidance.

We all need mentoring, but we can also be mentors. *You* could be the Titus 2 woman of someone else's prayers. No matter how inadequate we feel, we have skills and character traits someone else admires. God never intended for us to do mothering alone. We need to open our eyes to the resources around us and open our hearts to other moms needing our wisdom and support.

M&M's *from* the Bible Share

Lois was Eunice's mother, and Eunice was the mother of Timothy, the young pastor the apostle Paul personally mentored and wrote encouragement to in 1 and 2 Timothy. Lois was a devout Jewess who diligently taught her daughter the Old Testament Scriptures, and they both became Christians when Paul taught in their town. Together they raised Timothy to become a godly man and pastor: "That precious memory triggers another: your honest faith—and what a rich faith it is, handed down from your grandmother Lois to your mother Eunice, and now to you!" (2 Tim. 1:5 *The Message*).

Let's Talk about It

1. What is the hardest part of being a mom?
2. What has helped you the most during your parenting years?
3. How are you countering the world's ways and setting the moral compass in your home?
4. Who influenced you the most as a mother?

Mothering Special Needs Children and Children with Illnesses

Moms with a special needs child or an ill child say their two lifelines are *first* the Lord and *second* a mentor who appreciates the emotions and hardships of this parenting season. They also know God wants them to mentor another mom coming up behind them in this journey.

Mentor Tips ....

If you have a child with special needs or illness, you know intimately the trials your mentee is experiencing and can offer the solace and hope she so urgently needs. Maybe your children have different disabilities or illnesses, but you can be an empathetic listening ear, prayer partner, shoulder to cry on, and a safe place to unload pent-up emotions and fear. Be careful not to spend all your time together focusing on the hardships. Help her embrace the joys in life and in the Lord. Beware of her slipping into depression, fear, anxiety, or isolation. Remind her often that her child is beautiful in God's sight, and this is a kind response to use when she encounters inquiring eyes or insensitive words.

The mother of a Down syndrome syndrome child says information and support are the best help a mentor can provide. "My biggest piece of advice is to stop asking new parents of a special needs child or an ill child what questions they have or how you can help. Educate yourself and just do something. They're too overwhelmed to know what to ask, how to ask it, or what they need." Help your mentee see the following:

- No one expects her to be a perfect parent and have it all together.
- She needs to take time to refresh and refill.
- She must keep physically, mentally, and spiritually fit to stay healthy and strong.
- A support group offers many benefits.
- It blesses others to let them help her.

Mentee Tips

If you don't have a mentor, find one. Asking for help is *not* a sign of weakness. Acknowledge that this is hard and you can't do it alone; no one expects you to—especially not God.

The temptation is to focus on trials and difficulties, but let your mentor guide you into the peace of knowing how much God loves you and your child. Think about how God will use your child to draw others closer to Christ—maybe at doctors' offices, therapy, school, and church, or with neighbors and other moms. Look for ways your family can be a witness: "Yes, this is difficult, but with God's strength, we're doing it with joy."

God's Perspective: Search the Scriptures Together

- Every person is beautiful in God's sight—Ps. 139:14
- God created us to help each other—Eccles. 4:9–10
- Let God be your source of strength—2 Cor. 12:9

A Mentee Shares—*Kimberly M. Drew*

Having a child with special needs is challenging and rewarding. My husband and I were only twenty-two when we had our first child. A traumatic delivery caused multiple handicaps. Most of our friends weren't even married, and we were home with a helpless baby needing specialists and therapy five days a week. I had no time or emotional energy for relationships and suffered with isolation and depression—my marriage struggled. I didn't realize relationships were what I needed most for *my* healing process.

My husband became the youth pastor at his childhood church, and we had the children of a family with a disabled son, Monroe, attending our youth group. Monroe was older than Abbey was, but his mom Gloria knew what I was experiencing. She became a friend, a supporter, and a safe place to ask questions and vent without fear of judgment: "I can't take this one more day! I'm going crazy!" She hugged me when I needed to cry and told a funny story to one up mine when I needed to laugh. She has an amazing ability to mix compassion with reality, diffusing future fears.

She reads my face and asks how I'm doing. She understands before I even launch into the latest setback or heartache, and I have peace—I'm not alone. I can expect godly advice, prayer, and the affirmation I need to keep pressing on.

When Monroe passed away, Gloria mentored how to handle my biggest fear: losing Abbey. With a special medical needs child, every hospitalization and illness is a tornado of emotion. I saw Gloria live out God's sufficiency to handle those emotions. She was incredibly kind to the hospital staff and doctors. She was grace, strength, and brokenness all at once. She was honest about the pain and cried freely and openly.

Through it all, she held firmly to her belief that God is good, he loves her and her family, and he would get them through this. She showed I don't need to panic every time Abbey gets sick. God is able. He's enough. I've seen this to be true in Gloria's life.

My story with Gloria didn't end when she lost Monroe. She continues to be everything she was before, and has added a new role: fellow adoptive mom. Gloria adopted all her children, and we recently adopted a baby girl born prematurely and addicted to drugs. Gloria is my biggest supporter and cheerleader!

As I've become a seasoned mother raising a special needs child, I reach out to other young moms walking this road with me. We're all at different emotional and spiritual places in handling our child's diagnosis, but we can relate in a way no one else can. God has given us the gift of fellowship with other believers as a way to support and spur each other on in faithfulness to him. It's more than just tips and tricks on how to handle school, or deal with a physical or behavioral challenge . . . this kind of intentional fellowship and mentorship allows us to press through the trials of raising our children with special needs so we can experience the *joy* of Christ in doing it.

A Mentor Shares—*Lynda Young*

"All I hear from his teachers is, 'Jacob doesn't sit still.' 'Jacob doesn't finish anything.' I'm so frustrated, and he seems so sad all the time." Mom Carol shared her frustration as her six-year-old son squirmed in his chair.

"I remember those days with a hyper little son," I said. "I later learned his brain yelled to keep moving. I've also taught many wiggly, distracted little guys. They can't help it and usually end up in trouble. I love your son, and we can work on this together."

Carol smiled, leaned over, hugged me, and the tears flowed.

When you're exhausted and alone, you need someone to come alongside and mentor you to give you courage and hope. Especially someone who survived and whose son, now an adult, thrived.

I worked out a plan with Carol: Talk to his teacher and pediatrician about getting him tested for ADD/ADHD. Discuss pros and cons of drugs to help his brain focus. Cut out sugars and dyes, and check for allergies. Write what your family does in fifteen-minute segments.

Carol spent the next week journaling what times Jacob spent on exercise, play, video games, and bedtime routines. Seeing how he reacted to regular day activities provided clues of what to change. We set up times to connect. Texting worked best for daily check-ins, and getting together once a week helped with needed hugs, discussion, and prayer. We prayed for specific issues, and I offered resources to encourage Mom and the entire family.

Gradually, we saw changes. Having been through challenging situations in my own family brought Scripture to life, which I could share with Carol.

M&M's *from* the Bible Share

When a nurse was fleeing with the young grandson of King Saul, she accidently dropped him, and he became a special needs child and adult. But King David showed unprecedented kindness and mercy on him, and instead of living a handicapped life, he was treated like one of David's sons, even though the custom of the day was for the new king to kill all claimants to the throne (2 Sam. 9:10–13). A helpless cripple and a self-proclaimed "dead dog," Mephibosheth became part of a royal family. God shows his grace to all spiritually crippled sinners and offers us a place at his table with an eternal inheritance.

Let's Talk about It

1. Does your church have support groups for families with a special needs or ill child? If not, what steps could you take to start one?
2. How would spiritual fortification help a mother of a special needs or ill child cope with the potential hardships?
3. Why might a mom isolate herself?
4. How could a mother denying her own needs be detrimental to her child and family?

Mothering Prodigals

I was a prodigal who raised a prodigal. In *Praying for Your Prodigal Daughter*, I define a prodigal as a child breaking the heart of his or her parents—and of God. Having a prodigal doesn't make you a bad parent, but ignoring or condoning your prodigal's bad behavior does. We may not be able to change our child's behavior, but we can change our reaction to it, and we can pray for God to change our child. If you have a child rebelling against what God teaches in the Bible, you have a prodigal, and it hurts. But just because you love the child, it doesn't make his or her wayward or sinful behavior acceptable; it's still wrong. Sin is sin (Isa. 5:20).

Accepting that our child is a prodigal is painful because we fear it might reflect on our parenting. Sometimes it does. We need to prayerfully scrutinize our own actions and make changes God reveals—being in a mentoring relationships helps to do that. No one benefits from ignoring or condoning prodigal sinful behavior. A mentor willing to give honest feedback from her own experiences with her prodigal provides wisdom and insight into parenting a prodigal. (See also Tween and Teen Season in Chapter Eight; Young Adults Season in Chapter Nine; and Abuse/Addiction/Criminal Activities, Gender Identity Issues and Sexual Integrity, and Post-Abortion Recovery in Chapter Thirteen.)

Mentor Tips ....

Your mentee's child may have behaviors different from what you experienced with your own prodigal, but you can empathize with her heartache and pain. Perhaps you took specific actions you can share and admit mistakes she can avoid. But right now, she needs a pillar of faith . . . a listening ear . . . and a cry, a laugh, and a prayer partner.

In the Appendix and in *Praying for Your Prodigal Daughter*, I discuss personalizing and praying Scripture. Together find passages in the Bible to pray God's will for her child, and start with those in the God's Perspective: Search the Scriptures Together section that follows. Also, encourage her to journal her feelings. Remind her God forgives the sinner who accepts Jesus as Savior, repents, turns from sinful ways, and asks for forgiveness. Pray with her for her child to make a decision to become a forgiven child of Christ or to rededicate her life to Christ.

Mentee Tips ··

My heart breaks for you—I have a window into your pain. How could the child you love, pray for, cherish, and nurture, be doing and saying things so hurtful to watch and hear? Your mentor probably knows just how you feel and wants to be a source of support and encouragement during this troubling time. You can be honest and vulnerable. Her role isn't to judge, but to offer love, hope, and help.

God's Perspective: Search the Scriptures Together

- Show your child unconditional love without condoning behavior—Rom. 12:9–10; Eph. 4:15
- Know when to set boundaries—Matt. 5:37, 19:18–19; Mark 3:25
- Pray for God's will and purpose in your child's life—Ps. 55:17; John 8:32; Rom. 12:2, 8:28
- Pray for salvation and repentance—John 3:16; Acts 3:19, 26:17–19
- Don't let a prodigal destroy your family and marriage— Matt. 12:25

A Mentee Shares—*Heather B.*

A friend at work invited me to a women's Bible study. Little did I know my life was about to change. Growing up, I went to church, but I turned prodigal for fifteen years. The lady hosting this Bible study isn't perfect, but she reads, studies, believes, and walks out the Bible. And when she teaches, you listen. I'd never read the Bible, much less paid attention to a Bible teacher who speaks the truth.

When my husband told our prodigal daughter she had to leave, I was devastated. Surely, this woman would say he was crazy and I should divorce him. She took me straight to God's Word in Ephesians 5:22–24, where I'm to submit to my husband. Really?! Even concerning my child? Yep! It was a turning point in my marriage. When I submitted to my husband's decision, he changed toward me. It was so hard, but so worth it.

A Mentor Shares—*Heidi McLaughlin*

I'm at a season of life when God has given me enough pain, wisdom, and, ultimately, freedom and joy that need passing on to our next generation. I've mentored a patchwork of marvelous, eager, but broken and lost women who desire to be better wives, mothers, sisters, and daughters. Sadly, I notice a broken thread throughout each of their stories—a dysfunctional relationship with their mothers. This grieves me, because these women and their mothers are Christians desiring to live Christ's way.

I teach my beloved mentees about a command and a promise: "Honor your father and mother. This is the first of God's Ten Commandments that ends with a promise. And this is the promise: that if you honor your father and mother, yours will be a long life, full of blessing" (Eph. 6:2–3 TLB).

They ask, "How do I honor my mother who doesn't approve of me or how I raise my children, or tries to control me, or makes unrealistic demands, or is emotionally distant, and shuts me out?"

As they struggle through the first step—forgiveness—I teach them to *respond*, not *react*, to hurtful words or actions. I explain: When we *react*, our immediate emotions show our disapproval. When we *respond*, we stop to re-evaluate our feelings and formulate our response with *respect*. A healing tool is to write a letter to Mother expressing a desire for a loving relationship, to confront difficult issues, and to restore the relationship. When the mentees send me a draft, if it doesn't express love and respect, the letter goes back for editing.

Often, the healing and restoration come with the heart release of hurt, anger, and sometimes shame, expressed with vulnerability and honesty. When I take the time to prayerfully walk alongside these mentees and listen to their pain and struggles, they aren't walking this journey alone.

M&M's *from* the Bible Share

You probably know the story in Luke 15:11–32 of the prodigal son who broke his father's heart. He demanded his inheritance at a young age, left home, and squandered everything on sinful behavior until he was destitute and homeless. In shame, he returned home to his father, who welcomed him with a celebratory party. But the good brother, who stayed home and honored his father, was angry the prodigal received such a grand homecoming. The father assured this son that he was loved, "You are always with me, and everything I have is yours. But we had to celebrate and be glad, because this brother of yours was dead and is alive again; he was lost and is found."

If there are other children in your family, they may feel all your attention, time, and resources are going toward your prodigal. They also need attention, time, and love. Include them when praying for your prodigal.

Let's Talk about It

1. Why is it hard to share with someone about your prodigal?
2. What are some benefits of being a mentor, even if your prodigal is still a prodigal?
3. What steps can you take to protect the rest of the family?

4. Describe the effects a prodigal can have on the parents' marriage.

Single Mom

As a single working mom for seventeen years, I know this season well. The ideal is Mommy and Daddy raising a family together, but in today's era of divorce, single women having babies or adopting, and widows, many women parent on their own—not an easy undertaking. It feels like a constant juggling of time, energy, and finances.

Mentor Tips ....

The principles of single parenting are similar to those in the Mothering season of this chapter (see the tips on page 151), except everything is harder. Your role isn't babysitter or backup parent, but to help your mentee learn how to manage on her own. In your initial meeting, ascertain where she needs the most guidance.

- Balancing finances and paying bills?
- Finding time and energy to work *and* enjoy family?
- Making household decisions?
- Disciplining children?
- Dating?
- Loneliness?
- Grief? Anger? Frustration?
- Finding personal time?

If you are, or were, a single mom, share how you manage (or managed) this season. Even if you're not a single mom, remind her God is her heavenly Husband. Staying close to God will provide support and strength if she lets God, and you, help her. Encourage her to participate in a single parents, group at church or to serve with her kids at church so they *all* can make godly friends. Invite her to sit with you during church—it's lonely sitting by yourself while the kids are in Sunday school.

Mentee Tips ....

It can be scary and lonely trying to parent on your own. Evaluate the areas where you could use suggestions and guidance from a mentor, and start with the most urgent ones. A mentor provides someone to pray with and ask what God taught her during her single parenting years. She can't make everything right in your world, but she can lead you to the One who can.

Looking to the world for solutions may seem tempting and convenient, but the world's ways *always* lead to disaster and devastation. I wish someone had told me . . . and I had listened. Take your family to church and get them involved in youth activities. Seeing two-parent families may be difficult, but God wants you and your children doing life with a community of believers. Raising godly children on your own is much easier then raising ungodly children.

God's Perspective: Search the Scriptures Together
- God is your heavenly Husband; Let him fill the void in your life—Isa. 54:5
- God will help; you can do it!—Phil. 1:18–19, 4:13

A Mentee Shares—*Lisa B.*

I've been a single mom since I was twenty-three, raising my now thirty-six-year-old daughter alone, and then raising, since birth, her daughter she had at fifteen. Before my daughter got pregnant, I was born again but didn't commit. I loved the Lord, but loved doing life my way more. I knew something had to change and rededicated my life to following Jesus Christ.

I began attending church again, where I met Diana while attending her weekly Bible study. She quoted Scripture effortlessly. I would say, "I can never do that!" To which she would stamp her tiny foot, "Yes, you can, because you can do all things through Christ who strengthens you!"

The first Scripture she gave me to memorize was Joshua 1:8 (NKJV), and I personalized, "For this book of the Law will not depart from my mouth but I will meditate upon it day and night. For when I purpose to do all that is according to it, I will find my way prosperous and have good success in life." I researched the meaning of "meditate" and began memorizing Scripture, which saved my life and the life of my granddaughter I'm raising. I had no idea Diana was mentoring me, but I see now she was a Titus 2 woman teaching and training me. Diana is with our Father, and I cannot wait to see her again.

A Mentor Shares—*Lisa B.*

What my mentor Diana taught paved the way for me to mentor others. The many hard times of being a single parent graced me with understanding and insight into the hearts and lives of women I met along my journey. Often, I thought we'd be friends forever, but sometimes the mentoring lasted only a short season.

I found a book on mentoring by Janet Thompson and devoured it, wanting desperately to start a mentoring ministry in my church. It took years to understand I didn't need a formal ministry to mentor, because the many women God brought to me often wouldn't grace the doors of a church. Much of what we learn in life isn't in classrooms and books, but through the heart of another. The greatest joy is seeing growth in someone you help grow closer to God. Then even after being a mentor, sometimes we become a mentee again in a new season.

M&M's *from* the Bible Share

A poor, single-mom widow reached out for help:

> The wife of a man from the company of the prophets *cried out to Elisha*, "Your servant my husband is dead, and you know that he revered the LORD. But now his creditor is coming to take my two boys as his slaves."
>
> Elisha replied to her, "How can I help you? Tell me, what do you have in your house?"
>
> "Your servant has *nothing there at all*," she said, "except a small jar of olive oil."
>
> Elisha said, "Go around and *ask all your neighbors* for empty jars. *Don't ask for just a few.* Then go inside and shut the door behind you and your sons. Pour oil into all the jars, and as each is filled, put it to one side."
>
> She left him and shut the door behind her and her sons. They brought the jars to her and she kept pouring. When all the jars were full, she said to her son, "Bring me another one."
>
> But he replied, "There is not a jar left." Then the oil stopped flowing.
>
> She went and told the man of God, and he said, "Go, sell the oil and pay your debts. You and your sons can live on what is left." (2 Kings 4:1–7—emphasis added)

Single moms can learn from this story to ask for, and humbly receive, help from others and from God. Never underestimate God, who fed

5,000 with five loaves of bread and two fish (Mark 6:37–41). If the widow had asked neighbors for more empty jars, the olive oil would've kept flowing. Include your children in domestic chores, helping solve problems, praying, and praising God for his provision.

Let's Talk about It

1. Where do you go to meet other godly single parents?
2. What do you struggle with the most?
3. Where do you have a need only God could provide?
4. How can God use you to help other single moms?

Stepmom

I'm very familiar with this season, since my husband and I blended our families twenty-four years ago. I have one daughter, and he has two daughters and a son. When we first married, I read several Christian books on blending families and being a stepmom. I desperately needed a mentor's assurance that I was going to survive this difficult season. But there was no mentor stepmom sipping coffee across the table providing tips, answering questions, laughing, crying, and praying with me. The chair was empty, but it's been a blessing to fill that chair for many new stepmoms.

Even though our four children were teenagers, becoming a family wasn't as easy as I expected, and I made mistakes. We all bring baggage from our nuclear families into our blended families, and usually former spouses add to the relationship mix. A hard lesson to learn was we would *never* be a nuclear family. The second lesson sustaining me all these years, as we've become a loving, functioning family, has been to lower my expectations and be satisfied with however God works out situations.

Mentor Tips ....

As you relive the story of blending your own family, share helpful hints and mistakes to avoid, but be cautious of elaborating on your own story and minimizing your mentee's circumstances. Or if you portray becoming a stepmom as super easy, your mentee might feel you can't relate, or her situation is worse than she thinks, or she must be a bad stepmom.

- Listen empathetically to her struggles, but help her focus on the blessings.
- Encourage her to lower expectations. Teach her to pray and relinquish control of outcomes and circumstances to God.
- Keep her accountable to not trying to replace her stepchildren's biological mom, badmouthing her, or getting in the middle of their relationship. Show her how to create a new and different relationship with her stepchildren.
- Suggest she discuss with her husband and the kids what they should call her. If their mom is deceased, "Mom" might be appropriate. Or maybe they should just use her name.
- Brainstorm ways for the kids to introduce her that work for everyone. This experience is as new and awkward for the kids as it is for her.
- Guide her in praying for each member of the new family, including ex-spouses, even those causing trouble.
- Pray with her for each child individually and all the children's relationships.
- Teach her to pray for her marriage. Help her have compassion for her husband's guilt over his children's division between two families, possible difficult dealings with an ex-wife, and a multitude of other issues.
- Remind her not to put her husband in a position of choosing between her and his kids. A united and loving marriage

is best for *everyone*. Discuss ways for her to be his helpmate and teammate in blending their family. Help her focus on the future.

- Guard her against showing favoritism to her own children.
- Share what helped you.
- Don't try to fix her issues.
- Advise her to respond as a godly woman, wife, and mom.
- Help her accept that stepchildren have another set of rules, eating habits, and maybe even spiritual practices at their mother's home. The goal is for the kids to accept and adjust to your mentee's home procedures and practices, but give them time. She can't take their behavior personally if they rebel. They're just kids. She must pick her battles.
- If her children have a stepmom, help her learn to accept what she cannot change, and pray for her children when they go to their father's home.

Mentee Tips ....

Assuming the role of stepmom can seem daunting, but it can also be a blessed extension of your mothering role. Every new relationship takes time to develop and mature. This is new unchartered territory, and as a godly mom and wife, you want to extend grace whenever possible and allow everyone time to adjust. What worked for your mentor might not work for you, but pray before discounting her suggestions and let the Holy Spirit guide you.

God's Perspective: Search the Scriptures Together
- We're all God's children—1 John 3:1
- Seek peace and avoid strife in your blended family— Matt. 5:9
- Create a welcoming atmosphere in your home—Mark 10:14; Luke 18:16

- Look beyond the earthly family to creating a spiritual family—Matt. 12:48–50
- Patiently wait on God to unite your new family—Ps. 62:1–2; John 13:34–35

A Mentee Shares—*Heidi McGlaughlin*

I didn't have a mentor when we became a blended family. Both of our spouses died, so there wasn't anger and rejection, just a *lot* of grief. My plumb line in this new, complicated, and eclectic family was, and still is, Romans 15:7: "Accept one another, then, just as Christ accepted you, in order to bring praise to God." I didn't become a Christian until thirty-two; if Christ accepted me with all my junk, I had to treat my new family members the same way. That profound verse became foundational in every aspect of my life. Blending a family has been an amazing journey—my oldest stepdaughter calls me Mom.

A Mentor Shares—*Laura Petherbridge*

"Being a stepmom is so much harder than I expected," two-year stepmom Jessica admitted. I hear this often as a stepmom of thirty-one years and a mentor and life coach for stepfamilies. With each stepmom, the initial goal is to help her recognize "normal" for stepfamily living, which is typically revolutionary because she assumed the issues were unique to her situation. Revealing what thousands of other stepmoms experience often brings her a sigh of relief and a huge release from her shame. No stepmom wants to be the wicked stepmother, but many feel like one.

The second step is to help her embrace the uncontrollable—the choices of the other home directly affect her home. "Jessica, I need you to repeat after me out loud, 'I cannot control what goes on in the other home.' Repeat this phrase as often as needed to maintain your dignity." Relating to her pain allows the mentee to relax and reveal her true feelings. Around others she wears a mask—inside she's dying. Becoming a stepmom ushers in unexpected loneliness, fear, and insecurity.

Then she takes a leap of trust and whispers a secret not shared with even her closest friend: "I know I should, but I don't love my step kids the same way I do my own. I'm a wicked stepmom, aren't I? How can I be a Christian and not love my husband's kids? I want to . . . I just don't know how."

Now real mentoring comes into our relationship as I assure her I understand; she's not wicked, and what's she's experiencing is normal. Then I share how God taught me to love my stepsons through a long, difficult journey of pursuing the bond. I chose love when they resented me, forgiveness when they hurt me, and relationship when they might not want one.

The utmost mentoring gift I offer a sister stepmom is to assist her toward the Savior, who can teach her how to love and show compassion and kindness to a stepchild who might never love or embrace her in return.

M&M's *from* the Bible Share

Sarah—wife of Abraham, stepmother to Ishmael, and birth mother to Isaac—is an example of how *not* to act as a stepmother. Sarah was jealous of Abraham's attention to Ishmael. She treated her stepson horribly and forced Abraham to abandon Ishmael and his mother. The two stepbrothers' feud and rivalry continues today through their descendants in the Middle East (Gen. 16–17, 21).

Let's Talk about It

1. How do the roles of birth mom and stepmom differ?
2. How could a bad relationship between a stepmom and her stepchildren affect her marriage?
3. What are some ways for a stepmom to get along with her stepchildren's mother?
4. Why are stepmoms portrayed negatively?

Stay-at-Home Mom and Homeschooling Mom

Not all stay-at-home moms homeschool, but most homeschooling moms are stay-at-home moms. While there may be differences in their reasons for staying at home, they often share a feeling of isolation and missing contact with the outside world. A mentor can help restore balance and joy to the calling of a mom available to her children 24/7.

Mentor Tips ....

Arranging times to get together requires flexibility if your mentee has young children. You may find it best to meet in the evening when her hubby is home to watch the kids, or while the kids are napping or playing outside. If your mentee is a homeschooling mom, and you've had this experience, you can offer her a wealth of information. Keep in mind she may be using a different curriculum than you used.

Some stay-at-home moms struggle with depression from not getting out of the house—at least not alone—or not participating in social activities or adult interaction. She might appreciate help with organization skills, balancing time to spend with the Lord, and finding peace in her chosen parenting role. She'll greatly appreciate times when just the two of you go out for coffee, a meal, a walk, prayer, or women's ministry activities.

Mentee Tips ....

Some homeschooling moms find it beneficial to join a homeschooling group and seek out a mentor who has been homeschooling longer or, like Carrie A. in the A Mentee Shares section, look for a homeschooling or former-teacher mentor in your church.

A stay-at-home mom can benefit from time spent with a current or former stay-at-home mentor mom who can empathize with your experiences and frustrations while helping you find ways to enjoy and maximize this season. Please don't expect your mentor to be a grandmother or auntie to your children or a babysitter so you can get out. She may kindly offer to help occasionally, but don't be offended if she doesn't, and don't take advantage of her if she does. Her role is to guide you to a closer walk with God in your current life season . . . and then everything will look doable. *Every* mom benefits from a godly mentor who guides her in raising godly kids.

God's Perspective: Search the Scriptures Together

- Life can get hectic—Phil. 4:6–7
- Don't isolate yourself; make time to meet with others, not just moms—Heb. 10:24–25
- The fruit of the Spirit helps keep balance in a day— Gal. 5:22–23

A Mentee Shares—*Carrie A.*

Mentoring has changed my life. I probably wouldn't be walking with God, or still married, if it weren't for godly mentors—especially Janine, my spiritual mother who stepped up to the challenge of mentoring and loving me. I don't think Janine knew what she was getting into when I approached her on a Sunday morning to ask if she would mentor me, after pastor preached a sermon about mentoring. I wanted a Christian mentor who was also a seasoned homeschool mom to teach and encourage me in homeschooling and my Christian walk.

I've learned so much from Janine, but not because she has great words of wisdom—although she's wise and has an impressive gift of discernment. And not because she has it all together—she has faults that make her real, approachable, and relational. She doesn't like confrontation; yet she never backs down from confronting me.

Janine's best mentoring quality? She *lives* what she teaches and loves me unconditionally. I pray someday to become a mentor like Janine!

A Mentee Shares—*Lindsey Bell*

Two days before my first child was born, I quit a job I loved to stay home. I assumed I would love everything about being a stay-at-home mom. What I failed to realize was not everything about being a stay-at-home mother is glorious. Think poop explosions, never-ending messes, and lack of interaction with anyone over the age of five.

Mentoring encouragement from other women who had been there and lived to survive the chaos got me through those tough moments. They reminded me that not loving *everything* about being a stay-at-home mom doesn't make me a bad mom, or mean I love my kids any less. I'm just like every other mom: normal.

A Mentor Shares—*Esther*

I invited two young couples from church to dinner, and the wives, April and Mary, became my mentees. When Mary had her first baby, we didn't meet for a while, and then we met to do a study on Ephesians. Later, as babies kept coming, I met with them individually at their houses.

April wanted to homeschool her daughter, but with no experience and a resistant child, she struggled. The three of us got together for lunch occasionally, and as we were discussing April's problem, Mary suggested a book her sister used to start homeschooling. Since I'd been a first-grade teacher, I offered to go to April's house three times a week for a month and work with getting her daughter used to sitting and learning. April is now entering her second year of homeschooling and loving it.

M&M's *from* the Bible Share

Lois and Eunice, grandmother and mother of Timothy, were stay-at-home and homeschooling moms. They taught Timothy from the Scriptures, and he became a protégé of the apostle Paul, who credited Lois and Eunice for Timothy's spiritual maturity (2 Tim. 1:5). Teaching your children God's Word is vital to their spiritual and intellectual growth, whether or not you homeschool. Give your children devotional materials and a Bible and teach them to have a quiet time with you.

Let's Talk about It

1. Do you find staying at home fulfilling or difficult?
2. If you homeschool, what are your reasons?
3. What sacrifices have you made?
4. How have your children benefited?

Working Mom Inside and Outside the Home

Unfortunately, rivalry often exists between moms who don't work and working moms—whether they work at home or out of the home. Going off to work every day might look like a glamorous life to the mom working at home trying to juggle kids and a home office, and vice versa. But each mom has challenges and blessings and wants to be a good mom. Moms need to stick together. It's hard enough being a mom without feeling scrutinized and criticized for the choices you make for your family.

I've been a working mom outside the home and a work-at-home mom—both have perks and problems. Working outside the home requires childcare and determining when your child is old enough to be home alone a few hours. Working at home means you can literally work around the clock, so you must create a schedule that balances family time with work projects. I didn't have a mentor during those years, but I'm sure my daughter wishes I did.

Mentor Tips

If you both work, you'll need to make adjustments and be flexible in finding times to meet. If you live near each other, an early morning or evening prayer walk combines exercise and mentoring—download the Bible on your phones and start with a scriptural reading to discuss. Try coffee on Saturday mornings or coordinated lunch breaks. Keep working at it. Help your mentee make meeting times, and her time with God, a priority on her calendar. Show grace, but maintain accountability.

Mentee Tips

On your calendar, highlight appointments with your mentor as high priority. Work and motherhood aren't easy. Let your mentor help you go from juggling to balancing life's responsibilities, because in juggling, eventually something drops. Don't try to have it all together in front of her. Her role is to help you find peace and joy in this season.

God's Perspective: Search the Scriptures Together

- Be a godly woman of principle at work and at home—
  Ps. 90:17; Col. 3:23–24

- God created work, but focus on *his* work—Ps. 104:22–24
- The Proverbs 31 woman was a godly and wise wife, mother, and entrepreneur—Prov. 31:24, 26–28

A Mentee Shares—*Lindsey Bell*

Balance is a constant struggle for a stay-at-home mother who also works from home as an author. If I'm not careful, family suffers. When my second book was being published, my kids were three and six, and I was struggling big time. A mentor spoke tough love: "Pull back from your writing ministry for a season and focus on the kids. Your kids are only this young once."

Ouch! Those words stung but were exactly what I needed to hear. I imagine it was hard to tell me what she felt God leading her to say. But because she chose to say those hard things—and had earned that place in my life—she changed my life. Someday, when I'm in a different season and have more time to write, I'll be a better writer because of her too.

A Mentee Shares—*Tahni Cullen*

As a young woman on full-time staff at a large church, I knew the value of professional development. I also knew the need for personal mentoring to balance the work of serving God's people with home life as a wife and mom of a young autistic son. I prayed to find someone who understood the worlds of working in ministry and special needs.

One day while talking with an older woman who served food for church volunteers between church services, I realized we clicked in unexpected ways. She was the wife of an interim pastor; while raising a family they had moved from church to church, helping congregations heal amid transition. Sadly, at age sixty-two, her vibrant, intelligent, faith-filled husband developed early-onset Alzheimer's, which now, nearly twelve years later, had greatly advanced. As we exchanged stories, it became evident we were facing some of the same things: me with my young son, she on the other side of a life-span with her husband.

I reached out to see if she would mentor me for six months. She shied away from the word "mentor," feeling she didn't have much to offer with my job. But, as I listed the reasons why I chose her, she agreed to be my "special friend."

Our coffee meetings, along with her prayers and frequent cards of encouragement, lifted me at just the right times. As she shared stories of her experiences, hardships, and triumphs, with a litany of enduring faith, I saw something beautiful cultivating in me. Mentoring isn't just about gaining an insightful edge within your profession, but about framing your inner strength with new perspective of the human experience.

Learning how to parent my special needs child through this friendship-mentoring relationship helped me realize I could mentor younger women. I grew a love for cross-generational mentorship. We have much to offer one another.

A Mentor Shares—*Esther*

One of my mentees is a homeschooling mom and an aspiring author. With young children, her writing time at home is precious. I was an English teacher, so when we get together, ideas and words fly. One day her computer crashed and she lost almost all her writing. Inconsolable, she cried for two days. Finally, her husband told her to call me. I had to use some tough love to help her get a grip. It isn't always easy being a mentor, but it's always a privilege seeing God at work.

M&M's *from* the Bible Share

We often joke about being Proverbs 31 "wannabes," and the impossibility of consistently being a wife and mom of *noble character* (Prov. 31:10–31). I think God included this lengthy description of a working mom and wife as a role model to strive toward in various seasons of life. Working moms aren't a new phenomenon. Since biblical times, moms have managed homes and worked inside and outside the home. Modern conveniences make keeping house so much easier now than when our ancestors had to make their own clothes, butcher meat, bake bread, harvest the fields . . . and yet, we often stress over "so many things to do." A study of the Proverbs 31 woman—a wife, mom, and entrepreneur—might be a good study to do together.

Let's Talk about It

1. How does your work affect your family?
2. What helps you balance work and family?
3. When and how do you find time to spend with the Lord?
4. Do you feel your identity is in being a mom, a wife, or in your work? Or something else?

Empty Nest Mom

Where did the time go? It seems like your children were just in pre-school, and now the last one is graduating high school and launching out into the world. You know he or she will do just fine . . . but what about you? What do you do now?

While raising kids, Mom can morph her own identity solely into that of a mom. The empty nest can create a huge void in her heart that resembles grief—she doesn't know who she is anymore. Not only is her nest empty, she *feels* empty. Purposeless. The house is quiet, there are only one or two places to set for smaller meals, groceries last longer, and there's no homework to help with or music or sports practices or events to attend. Some women relish this new season to focus on things *they* want to do: start a new career, hobby, or service project. For others, depression darkens each day: they feel unneeded. Many empty-nest moms resort to drugs, alcohol, affairs, divorce, pornography, shopping . . . anything to dull the pain and fill the void *only* God can soothe, heal, and fill.

We *never* stop being our children's mother, but God's plan is for parents to raise children to be *progressively independent* of us and *completely dependent* on Jesus. Our children are his divine gift for us to nurture into godly young adults. Now we prayerfully turn our children over to God to use for his purposes. We pray for their daily protection, choices, decisions, futures, and personal relationships with others and with Jesus, while we ask him where he wants to use us. We don't find identity in *our children*; we find identity in *our Savior*.

Mentor Tips ....

If your mentee is seeking a mentor during this season, she's probably struggling. Determine quickly her physical, mental, and spiritual status. She may just need to hear that you made it through this season and she will too, or she could be in a dangerous place emotionally. If she's already fallen into an addiction, depression, marriage problems, or unsafe behavior, help her seek outside guidance immediately. If she's married, tell her you need to speak with her husband, who may be unaware of the seriousness of his wife's problems.

A good way to help her refocus is finding something she enjoys doing to get her out of the house—a hobby, work, volunteering, ministry. Encourage her to serve others at church or in the community. The first step in *healing* ourselves is *helping* others.

Share with her what helped you. She needs empathy, not sympathy. The goal is to help her see that God has much more planned for her as she transitions to the next season of parenting so her children can begin to develop their own independence and future relationships.

Married empty nesters may need encouragement to restore the communication and romance with their husbands now that they have the house to themselves again. It could be time to make plans for a second honeymoon!

Mentee Tips

Tell your mentor how you feel and where you need help. Be honest with her about fears, frustrations, and the future. Remember that you're God's daughter and he allows you to live your life with gentle guidance, and now he will help you do the same with your children. The closer you grow in your relationship with God daily, the more you hear his purpose and plans for your next season of life.

God's Perspective: Search the Scriptures Together

- Our children are always God's gift, even when no longer in our home—James 1:17
- Motherhood is not our only life purpose—Rom. 8:28

A Mentee and Mentor Share—*Katie and Ellie*

Our girls are now college students—twenty, twenty-one, and twenty-three. Ellie and I are empty nesters, but *always* mothers and friends. We've spent the last eighteen years since God matched us as M&M's in the mentoring ministry, doing life together . . . praying, sitting in hospital waiting rooms, traveling back and forth to visit each other after we both moved to different states, learning from each other, and most importantly, sharing Christ with each other.

Our families are forever friends. Our husbands talk about their jobs, their kids, and church. Our girls will always be a part of each other's lives because they grew up together. (Read more of Katie and Ellie's mentoring story on page 149.)

M&M's *from* the Bible Share

Hannah struggled with infertility and desperately wanted children. She made a vow: "Lᴏʀᴅ Almighty, if you will only look on your servant's misery and remember me, and not forget your servant but give her a son, then I will give him to the Lord for all the days of his life, and no razor will ever be used on his head"(1 Sam. 1:11). When God granted her desire for a child, Hannah, realizing her son was a gift from God, gave the child back to God to grow up in the presence of the Lord (1 Sam. 2:21). *Our* children are *God's* children first.

Let's Talk about It

1. What's a mother's main role in raising children?
2. If married, how can you restore any marital intimacy neglected while raising kids?
3. How can you remain a healthy part of your grown children's lives?
4. What are the risks and repercussions of raising your children to be codependent on you?

CHAPTER THIRTEEN

A DIFFICULT SEASON

After the sudden and tragic death of my first husband, I remarried and became the mother and stepmother of a blended family of five children and nine grandchildren. I believe this qualifies me to walk alongside women and speak God's love, wisdom, and practical ways to thrive in this demanding and complicated life.

   —Heidi McLaughlin

Praise be to the God and Father of our Lord Jesus Christ, the Father of compassion and the God of all comfort, who comforts us in all our troubles, so that we can comfort those in any trouble with the comfort we ourselves receive from God. For just as we share abundantly in the sufferings of Christ, so also our comfort abounds through Christ.

   —2 Corinthians 1:3–5

A difficult season can happen at any age and encompass a wide array of circumstances: illness, crises, tragedy, hardships, grief, loss, confusion, lifestyle choices, sin . . . the list is endless. In this chapter, I've combined various difficult life experience seasons but clearly delineated them so you can find the area that best fits your M&M's situation. While exact life experiences may differ, the mentoring principles are similar.

Christians are to comfort those in trouble with the same comfort we received from God in our difficult season (2 Cor. 1:3–5; Phil. 2:1–2). God puts people in our path going through something we've experienced and survived with his help, and he expects us to reach out to them with the power of his love, healing, and forgiveness.

No one wants to hear in the middle of a crisis, "Everything happens for a reason." That may be true, but it's not comforting. However, many M&M's say a crisis brought them together.

As a mentor, you might have to relive your pain; but God wants you to share with your mentee how he will walk beside her, just as he did during your darkest time, and you'll walk with her too. We receive our greatest healing and help when we extend healing and help to someone else. You may feel you should stop mentoring during a difficult season, but other women need to see how we do life as Christians in the hard times. Your mentee will be watching closely to learn how she should respond *when*, not *if*, her hard time comes. No one escapes life's difficult seasons.

If you happen to be in a difficult season, don't isolate yourself or pull away from women who can help you. It may be embarrassing or humbling to talk about your crisis, but you need godly perspective and encouragement.

Illness and Health Issues—Yours or a Loved One's

The primary reaction to a health diagnosis—ours or that of someone near to us—is shock and then fear. Our mind races with questions: How will this affect my life? Will I (or they) live? Raw emotions run rampant. We desperately long to hear from someone with real-life experience, not just the doctor giving clinical information, studies, and statistics. Other times, we escape into denial, and talking to someone who has had what we just heard described makes it all too real. However, avoidance only postpones dealing with the inevitable reality—something is terribly wrong.

Mentor Tips ....

If your experience is with the same illness as your mentee, or her loved one, you can empathize with her. Or maybe your illness is different. Either way, here are a few precautions:

- Everyone's body reacts differently to illness and treatment.
- Keep your time together all about her. You can share some of your experiences, but don't try to oversee her treatment and procedure plan, unless to offer suggestions for making something easier or more comfortable.
- Don't share horror stories—yours or someone else's.
- Never contradict the doctor. You can recommend questions to ask the doctor or suggest a second opinion. Lead her to the Divine Physician for wise counsel and peace.
- If appropriate, offer to accompany her to doctors' appointments to take notes.
- Add diversity to your meetings so the illness doesn't dominate your times together.
- Pray for God to give you just the right scriptural readings to encourage her.

Even if you haven't experienced a similar illness, she still needs a godly woman in her life to offer an objective and spiritual perspective, prayer, reprieve, and respite.

Mentee Tips ....

If you already have a mentor, she'll know just how to pray for you, even if she hasn't had the same illness, because you have a history together.

If you don't have a mentor, ask at church for someone to pray with, and look for a support group at a local church or hospital. Or seek out a godly woman you admire for prayer and fellowship. A mentor can't give you medical advice, but she can help you find wisdom, courage, and peace from God, the Divine Physician.

God's Perspective: Search the Scriptures Together
- God wants to hear how we feel—Ps. 77:1
- Don't become discouraged—Prov. 18:14

- Don't be anxious—Ps. 139:23; Phil. 4:6–7

A Mentee Shares—*Your Author, Janet Thompson*

With my first breast cancer diagnosis, I had so many questions after the shock of hearing *cancer*. My doctor's office had a mentoring program they called a "patient advocate." Grace became my mentor/patient advocate. Grace was on the healing side of her breast cancer treatment, and even though our breast cancers and treatments were completely different, Grace was a Christian, so we were sisters in Christ and in breast cancer.

Grace understood where I was emotionally and would call with an encouraging scriptural passage or prayer at just the right times. We became good friends and continued to spend quality time together until she passed away unexpectedly from congestive heart failure. At Grace's memorial service, I spoke about Grace's incredible gift of time and love when I was at my weakest. It was a blessing for her family to hear how my "Grace Abounds" mentored me.

A Mentor Shares—*Your Author, Janet Thompson*

When we finally reach the healing side of an illness, we typically want to distance ourselves from it. We don't want to relive the pain, fear, anguish, and vulnerability. But the Lord put on my heart to use my breast cancer experience to mentor other women going through breast cancer, just like Grace mentored me. The Lord's call resulted in the privilege of writing the book I wished I had going through the ordeal, *Dear God, They Say It's Cancer: A Companion Guide for Women on the Breast Cancer Journey*. This book, dedicated to my mentor, "Grace Abounds," allows me to mentor, encourage, and spiritually walk beside thousands of breast cancer sisters.

M&M's *from* the Bible Share

The Bible tells of a woman bleeding for twelve years:

> She had suffered a great deal under the care of many doctors and had spent all she had, yet instead of getting better she grew worse. When she heard about Jesus, she came up behind him in the crowd and touched his cloak, because she thought, "If I just touch his clothes, I will be healed." Immediately her bleeding stopped and she felt in her body that she was freed from her suffering. (Mark 5:26–30)

Jesus doesn't *physically* walk among us today, so we can't touch his cloak, but he is *spiritually* among us so we can touch him through prayer and faith. Jesus told the woman "Daughter, your faith has healed you" (Mark 5:34). Our faith may not *physically* heal us, but it will *spiritually* free us from fear, worry, and anxiety.

Let's Talk about It

1. Is having a mentor during illness a new concept for you?
2. What is the value to a mentee when her mentor continues mentoring during her own illness?
3. How might a mentee be of help when a mentor is ill?
4. Why doesn't it always help to tell stories about others' illnesses, even if their results were good?

Infertility

One in six couples suffer with infertility—a subject seldom discussed in church. When I was writing *Dear God, Why Can't I Have a Baby?*, many women said the place they felt the loneliest was in church. Heart wrenching! God talked about infertility and the plight of the infertile woman numerous times in the Bible, so why would the church go silent on infertility? Mentoring and spiritual support are vital for a woman experiencing the heartbreak of infertility. Women are often reticent to talk about their childless pain. A safe mentoring relationship can help break their silence.

Mentor Tips

If you've experienced infertility, you can commiserate with your mentee; but if you now have children, either natural or adopted, you're living your mentee's dream. Be sensitive to possible jealousy and defensiveness. Also, remember that what worked for you might not work for her. Your role isn't to help her get pregnant or become a mom but to encourage and pray for her to avoid discouragement and marital problems, which can escalate during this stressful season.

If infertility wasn't an issue for you, it is painfully insensitive and inappropriate to tell her God is in control and that maybe he doesn't want her having children. Don't use Scripture or Christian clichés to make her feel worse.

Help your mentee discover God's peace and encouragement through delving into his Word and prayer. If she needs kind responses or to forgive someone for saying hurtful and insensitive things, in the Appendix under "Infertility" there's a link to "The Top Fifteen Things *Not* to Say or Do and *To* Say or Do to Someone Experiencing Infertility" and "Suggested Responses from *Dear God, Why Can't I Have a Baby?*," which would be an excellent book to read and discuss together.

Teach your frustrated and despondent mentee how to turn to God when she experiences depression, hopelessness, or whatever else the enemy throws at her.

Mentee Tips ·······························

Let your mentor know where she can help you the most. What issues are the hardest for you? Choose a mentor you trust to keep your confidence so you can be open and vulnerable with her. Be patient if she says or does something seemingly insensitive. Gently let her know a more loving way to communicate her thoughts and ideas.

God's Perspective: Search the Scriptures Together

- You're going to experience varied emotions—Rom. 12:15
- God hears you—Ps. 25:16
- Worry doesn't help—Prov. 12:25

A Mentee Shares—*Shannon*

Dear God, Thank you for the women willing to share with me the things that helped them in their infertility journey. I especially appreciate those who said, "Call me with any questions," and I did. It was comforting that someone else knew what I was going through and would take the time to answer my many questions. God, I hope someday I'll be able to help others as much as they've helped me. Please remind me to do so.[1]

A Mentor Shares—*Lindsey Bell*

Loneliness dominated the months following each miscarriage. During the seasons of grief, supportive family and friends listened well, but they hadn't experienced recurrent miscarriages. I *so* needed a mentor who had walked this road . . . someone who understood losing multiple babies and never receiving the longed-for child. Even though I didn't have a mentor through those years, *I can mentor* someone else. I share openly about our losses. Often, through the sharing of our own pain, God heals our hearts as he heals the hearts of others.

M&M's *from* the Bible Share

The Bible discusses infertile women: Sarah, Rachel, Elizabeth, Samson's mother. Samson's mother (Judg. 13:2–25) and Hannah (1 Sam. 1:1–28) both trusted God with their infertility. Unlike Sarah and Rachel, they didn't manipulate the situation. Doctors can provide medical solutions, but only God knows the exact plan he has for how and when you will become a mother, which might be completely different from what you expect . . . if you wait for his will to be done on earth as it is in heaven (Matt. 6:10).

Let's Talk about It

1. Why doesn't the church discuss infertility?
2. What other plans might God have for the mommy-in-waiting?
3. How could infertility affect a marriage?
4. What emotions might a husband experience?

Abuse, Addiction, and Criminal Activities

I grouped these seasons together because often a history of abuse results in addictions that lead to encounters with the law—or each season can stand alone. Mentors are *not* fixers; they *are* accountability partners, encouragers, and teachers of how to use God's truths found in the Bible to guide the mentee into living a virtuous, moral life.

Mentor Tips ....

This might not be an easy relationship depending on where your mentee is in her life. Stay strong and grounded in your faith—don't become an enabler! Your mentee needs lots of love and nurturing but also accountability and responsibility. If she's currently involved in abusive, addictive, or even criminal behavior, she must seek professional help. Remember, your role is mentor, not rescuer.

If your mentee is recovering from a wayward season, encourage her to join a Christian recovery program like Celebrate Recovery. You might want to attend with her in the beginning until she feels comfortable going on her own.

Don't try to tackle the multitudes of areas needing attention in her spiritual and personal life all at once. Start *first* with seeking God's forgiveness for her sins and mistakes and making a commitment to follow Jesus. If your mentee is a new believer or wants to become a believer or rededicate her life to Jesus, go to Chapter Seven, Seeker or New Believer Season. Then help her work on forgiving herself and others.

Foster care programs greatly need mentors. My friend Dianne was a big-sister mentor to a young troubled girl at a foster care facility. Dianne said, "I was told nobody had broken through to her. Questioning why I was even interested in her, for the first three weeks I sat patiently as she told me to leave or said something insulting. Then I asked if she'd like to go for a ride. She would shadow me on weekends to see life away from the orphanage."

But even with Dianne's mentoring, her mentee got involved with a man who became her pimp. I share this story because Dianne says she still has fond memories and stories of mentoring this troubled girl. You may not see a dramatic change in your mentee. Mentoring isn't about *you*; mentoring is about *her*. So don't feel like a failure if God lets you participate in her story but doesn't reveal the final chapter.

Many women's problems stem from past trauma that has damaged their self-worth, which starts a downward spiral of seeking validation and love. Your mentee's bad behavior is probably the result of something in her past, and as she builds confidence and trust in your mentoring relationship, pray God will reveal to you, and her, the root of her problems. Perhaps as she unravels those feelings and events, her life will turn around. Only Jesus can fill the hole in the heart of a woman seeking fulfillment and obliteration of pain through addictions, criminal activity, or subjecting herself to atrocities. Let her tell her story, but help her create a new Christ-centered life story.

Mentee Tips ....

If you surrender your life to Jesus and ask for his help, you *can* break free from the binding chains of abuse, addictions, or criminal behavior! Reread that sentence again with conviction: If *I* surrender *my* life to Jesus and ask for his help, *I can* break free from the binding chains of abuse, addictions, or criminal behavior!

Your mentor can't change the past, remove your desire or cravings, or rectify wrongs. She can't make everything right in your life, but she *can* help you learn to trust the one who provides peace, forgiveness, restoration, and wholeness: Jesus Christ. Let your mentor walk with you through this difficult transition time of repentance, forgiveness, and restoration in Jesus so someday you can mentor another hurting and troubled woman.

God's Perspective: Search the Scriptures Together

- Help overcoming a criminal past—Ps. 68:6, 142:7
- God offers new life and hope—Ezek. 34:22; Ps. 10:14, 146:7–8
- God can help overcome any addictions—1 Cor. 10:13

A Mentee Shares—*Tina* (As told by her mentor, Sheryl)

I met Tina when she entered the women's program at The Mission, where I volunteer. Tina was cautious, not willing to trust anyone; she had no sense of self-worth. An alcoholic and homeless, she lived on the streets, where she was gang raped and lost all her possessions. After a month in the women's program, the shock of detox threw her into relapse. Back on the streets, she drank herself into numbness and wandered aimlessly for weeks. Finally realizing she couldn't help herself, she went back to The Mission and asked to re-enter the program.

This time was different. She opened her heart to God's power and Word and willingly participated in the classes. She was honest about the areas where she needed healing, including sexual abuse. Tina could hardly discuss the unthinkable things that happened to her on the streets, yet knew she had to face her pain. She asked her teacher about the guilt and shame. "God sees you flawless, Tina. God loves you; He has forgiven you. You must accept his forgiveness and forgive yourself."

"That day," Tina says, "my recovery took a turn. I began believing God forgave me and felt free from guilt and shame. I'm so thankful for God's grace."

A Mentor Shares—*Sheryl* (Tina's Mentor)

I serve as a mentor at The Mission, a one-year residential program for women—both walk-in residents and court-ordered placements—to assist with rehabilitation and community re-entry for women incarcerated for crimes and offenses: child endangerment, alcohol and drug abuse, prostitution, and grand theft. The walk-in residents are usually homeless addicts or alcoholics who have lost everything—jobs, homes, families, dignity, and self-esteem.

During the last three months of the program, each resident receives a mentor. When I became Tina's mentor, our time together seemed like a couple of friends hanging out. The local Christian radio station where I work needed volunteers for events, and Tina was a willing hand and a big-hearted servant.

Sadly, shortly after Sheryl wrote this story, Tina relapsed again. Sheryl doesn't consider herself a failure. She still prays for Tina and knows she was part of Tina's journey—one she hopes will lead her back to rehabilitation and to God.

M&M's *from* the Bible Share

Rahab was a prostitute. She probably suffered abuse and maybe even used her profits to support an addictive habit. But when given the opportunity to change her life and trust God by hiding the Israelite spies scouting Jericho for future seize, God spared her and her family. "It was by faith that Rahab the prostitute was not destroyed with the people in her city who refused to obey God. For she had given a friendly welcome to the spies" (Heb. 11:31 NLT).

Rahab is a beautiful role model of how faith in God can restore a life and change the future. "Rahab the prostitute is another example. She was shown to be right with God by her actions when she hid those messengers and sent them safely away by a different road" (James 2:25 NLT). Just think . . . Rahab, the prostitute who chose to follow God by faith, became the great-great-grandmother of King David (Matt. 1:5–6).

Let's Talk about It

1. Why is it so hard to let go of our past?
2. How can someone stop an abuser from still negatively affecting her life even after the abuse has ended?
3. Why is staying free from addiction a daily process?
4. How could someone benefit from a Christian mentor, along with a rehab sponsor?

Gender Identity Issues and Sexual Integrity

Sin is sin, no matter what spin our culture puts on it. *Any* sex outside of marriage—casual, hookup, living together, adultery, friends with benefits, dating, homosexual, transgender, bisexual, or marriage not between a man and a woman—is outside of God's ways and his will. Regarding the LGBTQ agenda, Glenn T. Stanton, director of Global Family Formation Studies at Focus on the Family, explains:

> Gender identity does not exist in any objective or quantifiable sense. There is simply no physiological, legal, medical, or physical-appearance criteria that a transgender person must meet to be properly distinguished as such. The gay or transgender "reality" exists solely in the mind of the individual making the claim. This is unmistakably clear in HRC's [Human Rights Campaign] own definition of gender identity: "One's innermost concept of self as male, female, a blend of both or neither—how individuals perceive themselves and what they call themselves."[2]

Tucked away in the bottom corner column of a page in *Time* magazine, under "Being Transgender Is Not a Mental Disorder," was this study:

> A study published in *The Lancet Psychiatry* suggests that feelings about gender identity are not the primary cause of transgender people's mental distress, as has been widely believed; the distress stems more from their common experiences of social rejection and violence.[3]

With all the media and public attention, some children, teens, and even adults may think it's cool or trendy to be transgender or try life as the opposite sex.

Gay, transgender, gender identity, or sexual integrity issues are all spiritual disorders. A Christian mentor is invaluable in helping reveal and dispel Satan's lies that God didn't create humans either male *or* female and that sex isn't *only* for marriage between a male and female. If you're a woman suffering under sexual deception or temptation, something has caused you to identify with the gender opposite of the one God gave you, to have an immoral and lustful sexual attraction to your own gender, or to be sexually promiscuous. But your *desires* don't make sinful behavior right or normal (Isa. 5:20).

Every morning, I pray Dr. Charles Stanley's prayer from Ephesians 6:10–18, "Dressing in Your Spiritual Wardrobe." Under the Breastplate of Righteousness he writes, "Through this I guard my heart and emotions. I will not allow my heart to attach itself to anything impure. I will not allow my emotions to rule my decisions. I will set them on what is right and good and just. I will live today by what is true, *not by what I feel.*" Under the Sword of the Spirit, which is the Word of God, Stanley says, "Your Word is strong and powerful and able to defeat even the strongest of Satan's onslaughts. Your Word says that I am not under obligation to the flesh to obey its lusts. Your word says that I am free from the power of sin."

God is *not* the originator, supporter, or cheerleader of the LGBTQ movement or *any* sexual sin—Satan is. That might sound harsh, but there are only *two* spiritual forces in this world: God and Satan, good and evil. Historically, new generations want to rebel against the morals, values, and traditions of previous generations by doing something radically different, though often immoral and even evil. Sadly, previous generations have legalized abortion and abolished the sanctity of virginity and sexual purity, and today's generations are trying to eradicate genders. Tragically, these sins—even though legalized or normalized—actually rebel against a woman's own body and rebel against God.

Mentor Tips ....

In today's liberal culture, you may encounter a mentee who

- "Feels" gay, transgender, or bisexual
- Is unmarried and sexually active
- Is an adulteress
- Looks at pornography
- Is promiscuous or a prostitute
- Lives together with a sexual partner

Before you agree to mentor a woman engaging in any sexual sin, you *must* be clear on your own views of what constitutes sexual sin and be willing to uphold in a loving, but *doctrinal* way, what the Bible clearly delineates as immoral, perverted, and adulterous sexual behavior. Often this lack of sexual integrity stems from a past life circumstance or trauma, such as abuse, abandonment, bullying, loneliness, molestation, parental relations, insecurities, low self-worth, or fragile self-esteem. Something is at the root of this behavior. Even though premarital sex is considered "normal" by the world, it's still sexual sin in God's eyes and giving in to peer pressure or trying to fit in, instead of considering herself valuable enough to wait for marriage, still indicates a core problem to explore together.

Get to know your mentee and encourage her to tell you her story. Pray God gives you wisdom to hear the root of her current choices. Listen carefully for issues making her vulnerable to this lifestyle. If she has gender confusion and has started using a man's name, always address her by her birth name.

Be honest and forthright that following God is never about how we feel or what the world determines is okay or even legal, but *always* about the truth of God's Word, which you want to explore with her. Let her know you care about her as a person, but you *always* will mentor from God's Word, not the world's ways. Satan says she's gay, bisexual, or transgender, or tells her it's okay to have promiscuous sex—and if she gets pregnant, she should have an abortion or take a morning-after pill. God says he created her wonderfully and beautifully pure as a heterosexual female in God's image someday to unite sexually—yes, as a virgin—in marriage with a godly man, and every baby has a right to life.

Realistically, and tragically, today there are few virgin brides, but you can lead your mentee through a prayer of rededicating her spiritual and sexual life back to the Lord, her heavenly Groom. She can never reclaim her virginity, but God is a forgiving God, and she can vow to sexually sin no more from this moment forward.

Bible study is vital to helping unlock God's Word with her regarding God's views on sexual integrity, especially a study on spiritual warfare. Treat her as a whole person, not defined by her sexual identity, habits, or choices, but by her identity in Christ. Use the suggestions under Resources for Specific Seasons in the Appendix for further help and guidance. Don't lose hope, even if you see no change. Stay faithful to the truth. Look for these problem areas to address in her life:

- Lack of discernment
- Not knowing how to set boundaries
- Giving into temptation
- Troubled past
- Abandonment by, or bad relationship with, her father
- Codependent relationship with mother
- Diminished self-worth and self-esteem
- Anger

Mentee Tips

Your mentor won't condone anything contrary to God's Word and his ways, substantiated in the Bible. She won't agree with choices that go against God's plans for heterosexual relations in marriage between a man and a woman, moral sexual integrity, and the creation of male or female. Keep an open mind and open heart and let the Holy Spirit do his work through God's Word and your mentor.

God's Perspective: Search the Scriptures Together

- God creates gender and makes no mistakes, no matter how we "feel" about it—Gen. 1:27
- Being a God-created female is a blessing—Gen. 5:2
- God loves you, but he won't tolerate sin—1 Cor. 6:9–11
- If you choose to keep sinning, God won't stop you, but he never condones sin—Rom. 1:18–20, 26–28, 32; Col. 3:5
- We honor God when we treat our bodies as his holy vessel—1 Cor. 6:20
- Show self-control—1 Thess. 4:3–4
- God will help you resist every sinful temptation, if you let him—1 Cor. 10:13
- Learn what's right in God's eyes—Rom. 15:2
- Homosexuality is wrong; God created sex to be between a married man and woman—1 Cor. 7:2–4; 1 Tim. 1:9–11
- God mercifully calls you out of darkness—1 Pet. 2:9–11

A Mentee Shares—*Sally Gary*

In her memoir *Loves God, Likes Girls*, Sally Gary shares her struggle with same-sex attraction:

> We've all bought into lies about ourselves that direct the course of our lives in ways that God never intended for us. Depending on a host of factors that we experience, we will end up in different places, struggling with different temptations; but the base lies have all been the same. However, I believe wholeheartedly that replacing those lies with God's truth is in my best interest and is ultimately what will allow me to fully experience all that God wants to bless me with in this life.
>
> Our truest picture of self needs to come from God—a God who loved us enough to come down to live among us,

to live sacrificially alongside us, ultimately giving himself to die in our place. . . . Even in our most sinful state, we were worth the sacrifice, simply because we are God's children, his daughters, heirs to the throne, a chosen nation, a royal Priesthood. This is how Scripture describes us, giving us immeasurable worth to the God of the universe. If that's where my identity comes from, then the lies are, at the very least, uprooted.[4]

A Mentor Shares—*Ashley Chesnut*

A young single girl in our church contacted me saying she had questions about seminary and ministry, so . . . I thought that would be the direction of the conversation. But within minutes of sitting down at the table, she began pouring out her story and confessing her struggle with same-sex attraction, codependency, and how she had acted out physically with another girl. . . .

I admire her courage.

Sharing your junk with another person is hard enough, but same-sex attraction has become the modern scarlet letter in the church. So for this girl to tell someone she barely knew—especially a church staff member—that she struggles with same-sex attraction, and wants help in dealing with her sin, demonstrated to me that the Holy Spirit was definitely working in her life.

That conversation led to a discipling relationship, and for the past year, this girl and I have been meeting regularly. It has been a joy to see what God has done in her life, for she is *not* the same girl who verbally vomited her story to me last summer. God has *not* taken away her temptation—her attraction to other females, but He provides the grace and strength for her to resist temptation.

In a recent conversation, she acknowledged that she "feels dangerous." She fears forming friendships with other females her age because of the *chance* that she *might* be attracted to them. She fears slipping into old habits, of regressing. . . . Giving into this fear of "what if" isolates her from people, which is what Satan wants, for if we withdraw from biblical community, we remove ourselves from the very family of believers that God has provided to walk alongside us and to help us grow in Christlikeness.

God has been teaching me a couple of things as I have walked alongside her and a few other girls with similar stories. Primarily, I've learned the importance of being sticky. I'm not going to drop out of their lives because of their particular brand of baggage. Let's be real—we all have baggage. Some is just more prettily packaged than others. But people who risk being vulnerable with their baggage should know that we're not going to run away because of what they have shared with us.

For life change to happen, people need the Spirit of God, the Word of God, and the people of God. This girl needed someone willing to walk with her, not run away from her. Someone who would stick to her, no matter what she said or how she reacted. But we cannot be sticky if we allow fear or prejudice or our own comfort and convenience to keep us from engaging with sinners in the first place.

Second, sinners need *safe* people to walk alongside them. Are you someone to whom people feel safe confessing? Do they know that you won't be shocked or scared if they tell you that they have been looking at porn, having sex with another woman, masturbating, or questioning their gender identity? Do you contribute to sinners' "feeling dangerous," or do you create a space where they feel safe to show their brokenness and to lay it at the feet of Jesus?

Third, walking with sinners often puts you on a steep learning curve, but God keeps His promise to give wisdom to those who request it (James 1:5). I knew from the get-go that I wasn't supposed to drop out of this girl's life, but let me assure you that I was flying blind. It's not like I had a lot of prior experience in dealing with people who struggle with same-sex attraction. Throughout this whole process, I have done lots of reading, researching, and talking with counselors. But God has been just as gracious to me as He has been to this girl. He equips us to do what He calls us to do (2 Cor. 9:8).[5]

M&M's *from* the Bible Share

The only examples we have of homosexuality or transgenderism in the Bible are negative ones, because God is clear that any deviation from sex between a married woman and man is immoral and a sin (1 Cor. 7:2–5)—so much so that he wiped out the sinful cities of Sodom and Gomorrah, where perverse and homosexual behavior was prevalent. Sexual perversions aren't new; only the names man gives them are new, like *gay*, *gender identity*, *bisexual*, and *transgender*—politically correct words for what the Bible calls *perverse*, *immoral*, and *detestable*.

God does use Sodom and Gomorrah as an example of what happens when people continue living in sexual promiscuity and perversion:

And don't forget Sodom and Gomorrah and their neighboring towns, which were filled with immorality and every kind of sexual perversion. Those cities were destroyed by fire and serve as a warning [or example] of the eternal fire of God's judgment. In the same way, these people—who claim authority from their dreams—live immoral lives, defy authority, and scoff at supernatural beings. (Jude 7–8 NLT)

Let's Talk about It

1. Why are gender identity and LGBTQ issues so prevalent today?
2. How is helping someone resist sexual sin more loving than tolerating her sin?
3. Gay marriage is legal now, but what does God's law say about it?
4. How would you mentor someone considering sex-change surgery?

Post-Abortion Recovery

Sadly, many women suffer today from guilt, fear, anger, regret, depression, self-destruction, addictions, and a multitude of devastating repercussions from past abortions. They may wonder if God could forgive them and whether they can forgive themselves. What seemed like a quick and easy solution to her unplanned pregnancy at the time now haunts the woman, and probably will for the rest of her life. Mentoring can help her seek the peace and forgiveness her heart craves.

Mentor Tips ....

If your mentee is considering an abortion, whether she is married or single, see the Chapter Twelve seasons Teen Moms (even if not a teen) and Pregnancy—Planned and Unplanned for how to mentor someone considering an abortion. Also, review with her the consequences of her choices and the trauma women suffer for a lifetime after choosing abortion.

Your post-abortive mentee may not realize how deep her pain goes until you start meeting together and talking. It could take time for her to trust you enough to share her abortion story. Be sensitive—not judgmental or critical. She can't change the past, but you can help her recover from bad choices and make God-honoring choices in the future.

Patti Smith, who contributed to A Mentee Shares and A Mentor Shares in this life experience season, participates in post-abortion healing retreats, and she offers the following mentoring suggestions:

- Share your post-abortion healing experience first (if you have one) to establish a kinship and show her that if God forgave and restored you, he will do the same for her.
- She may have hidden this secret for fear of others thinking her stupid or evil—even you.
- Validate her emotions.
- Assure confidentiality.
- Focus on her asking forgiveness from God and anyone else hurt by the abortion.
- Help her go through the grieving process for her actions and her lost baby.
- If she's not married but is sexually active, talk about why God wants her to sexually abstain until marriage—the scriptural context for intimacy and pregnancy—and lead her in a prayer of rededicating her sex life to God.
- If she won't agree to abstinence, discuss how to *prevent future* abortions—stress that abortion is NOT birth control.
- If she's married and considering another abortion, take her to Isaiah 59:1: "Surely the arm of the LORD is not too short to save, nor his ear too dull to hear." When you make the right decision for your unborn baby, God will take care of you and the child.

Healing from abortion is ongoing. She may never completely forgive herself, but help her learn how to understand and receive restoring mercy and absolute forgiveness from God. Perhaps like Patti, some-day your mentee will use her story to help other women at a crisis-pregnancy center or pro-life organization—something you could do together. (See the Appendix for post-abortion retreat information.)

Mentee Tips ....

Try to find a woman who has experienced spiritual healing from abor-tion and is willing to mentor you through your post-abortion healing. Or look for a loving, compassionate Christian woman you respect to guide you through understanding and receiving God's forgiveness, grace, and mercy.

When you feel a bond of trust with your mentor, share your story and listen to her suggestions for getting in a right relationship with God and others. A natural tendency is to justify choices and actions, masking pain. God wants you to give your pain over to him.

God's Perspective: Search the Scriptures Together

- God's forgiveness is complete—Ps. 103:12; Isa. 43:25
- God is compassionate toward our mistakes—Mic. 7:19
- Go and sin no more—John 8:10–11

A Mentee Shares—*Patti Smith*

I struggled for decades with depression, alcoholism, and promiscuity. Through God's intervention, I became sober but remained emotionally disjointed. Then I converted to Catholicism and attended a seminar where tears flowed as a speaker shared her abortion experience. I felt God compelling me to attend a post-abortion healing retreat.

The leader, Rosemary, gently mentored us through the healing process, which included prayer, sharing, journaling, and education on how the trauma of abortion affected us emotionally and physically. The process revealed the source of our pain, anger, remorse, and fear, resulting in unsavory behaviors toward not only ourselves, but those we loved. By the end of the retreat, we came to terms with our abortions and were able to ask for, and accept, forgiveness from God, our lost children, and ourselves.

My grateful heart wanted to participate in helping with this wonderful ministry. It was a blessing to have Rosemary as a mentor once again, only this time in how to become an instrument of healing and mentoring to others.

A Mentor Shares—*Patti Smith*

Susan, a post-abortive woman facing a second unplanned pregnancy and considering another abortion, contacted me on Facebook. She was struggling financially and had other children to support. She worried her significant other wouldn't stand by her if she kept the child, and she knew her mother would be disappointed.

Our first contact, I was careful not to ask defensive questions like "Don't you use birth control?" I focused on her feelings after the last abortion. She said a little sad, but felt she had no choice. I shared my abortion story, which included an addiction to alcohol. She admitted abusing prescription medication, and then realized this was her way of covering up the pain of abortion. The floodgates opened as words rushed onto the screen: *anger, self-hatred, regret*. I suggested she deal with her substance abuse and find a healing program, and I provided some resources. I had her read back all she shared. Would she be willing to go through that pain a second time?

A few days later, she messaged she was stopping the pain medication to protect the baby. She decided to keep it and sign up for Rachel's Vineyard [an international healing program—see the post-abortion resources in the Appendix]. Susan promised to keep in touch, which she did. A month later, she miscarried and the guilt resurfaced. She felt God was punishing her for the last abortion. I assured her God wasn't vengeful, but full of love and mercy. We might not understand the whys, but if God were punishing her, she wouldn't have the beautiful children she gave birth to after her first abortion.

Our first online chat was two years ago. We stay in contact, and she's pregnant again with a little girl. I have a baby gift wrapped and ready to mail!

M&M's *from* the Bible Share

In the scene in John 8:10–11, Jesus was talking to a woman caught in the sin of adultery: sex outside of marriage. Sex between a male and female of any species often results in conception—all in God's magnificent design of procreation. When Jesus forgave the woman, he told her to stop having promiscuous sex: the leading cause of abortions.

Let's Talk about It

1. How can a mentee benefit from a mentor who has received God's redemptive forgiveness?
2. Why would a woman feel God were punishing her if she miscarried or couldn't get pregnant again?
3. Why is it hard for us to take responsibility for our actions?
4. What solace can a Christian post-abortive woman find in seeing her baby again someday?

Loneliness

Loneliness is the most common theme in the Woman to Woman Mentoring Ministry. Some are lonely as the only Christian in their family. Others have husbands who travel for work or are deployed in the military. Some are empty nesters and the house is too quiet, or they just moved, started attending a new church, or are stay-at-home moms with small children.

In our fast-paced world, we often don't know our neighbors. We become engrossed in our own lives and don't notice the lonely women around us desperate for fellowship with other believers in a personal setting outside of church. Ask God to show you a woman in your church, neighborhood, workplace, or community, or moms of your children's friends who could use a cup of coffee or tea and a chat. If that lonely woman is you, invite another woman in those same places to have coffee or lunch with you. We each have to step out of our comfort zone to overcome isolation.

Mentor Tips ....

Your mentee may just need a listening ear, so don't be surprised if she does all the talking at first. Your role isn't to fill her loneliness void by becoming her BFF or constant companion, but let her know you're someone she can count on to meet with regularly who cares about her and will pray with and for her. At first, you may need to do the following:

- Set boundaries.
- Introduce her to other Christian women so she can start making friends and building a support system.
- Find ways to help her get involved in her community and church—maybe join a Bible study or book club.
- Look for signs of depression that might require counseling or medical help.

- Let her cry. Tears are God's way of emotional release.
- Remind her Jesus is always with her, but you understand she needs "Jesus with skin on."

Mentee Tips ....

If you feel lonely, reach out to a woman at church or join a small group or Bible study to meet other Christian women. Loneliness is debilitating and demotivating—that's not where God wants you. Make a concerted effort to find a woman you admire spiritually and personally and ask her to mentor you. She probably will not become your best friend and do everything with you, but she can introduce you to other Christian women and help you draw closer to Jesus, who calls you his friend. You can count on your mentor to pray for you, be a listening ear, and share tips that helped her overcome loneliness.

God's Perspective: Search the Scriptures Together

- God has prepared for you a spiritual family in the church— Ps. 68:6
- God will never leave you—Heb. 13:5
- God is always with you—Matt. 28:20
- Jesus is your friend—John 15:13–15

A Mentee Shares—*Erica Wiggenhorn*

Five sleepless nights caring for a newborn and toddler—I needed help. Since we had moved, our two-year-old daughter screamed every night at bedtime and woke up throughout the night. I was a walking zombie.

One morning, I hopped into the shower before she and our infant son awoke. Desperate to make new friends, I had a neighborhood brunch to attend. We'd been in North Carolina less than two weeks; I missed my friends with a palpable ache. I fervently prayed to make a connection with someone at this brunch.

I nervously tapped on Starr's front door. Would Eliana behave? Would Nathan cooperate? I felt anxious, my emotions shredded and frazzled from exhaustion. Then a beautiful smiling woman answered the door and reached out her hand to Eliana, "I'm so glad you made it!"

After wonderful food and adult conversation, we loaded back up in the wagon and trudged home—refreshed. Until the bedtime nightmare began again. The next day, I called Starr. My intentions were to thank her for such a lovely afternoon, but I asked for something else . . . prayer.

I tearfully shared exhaustion from Eliana's not sleeping. Starr prayed over the phone and, a few minutes later, appeared on my doorstep. Mortified of my new neighbor witnessing our "newborn house," I invited her inside. We prayed in Eliana's room, asking for the peace of Jesus and the Spirit of God.

The next day, Starr showed up again: "I was praying for Eliana and for this retreat I'm preparing for, and the Lord gave me the most beautiful illustration." She reached into a bag and pulled out glow-in-the-dark stars. "Abraham could only see stars when he stood in the dark. Sometimes we have to go to dark places to see the glory and majesty of God! You helped *me* by asking for help. If you hadn't called, I still wouldn't know what to share tomorrow."

She put those glow-in-the-dark stars on the ceiling above Eliana's bed and told her, "When you look at those stars, remember Jesus is right here in your room, watching over you." Eliana couldn't wait to go to bed. Her night terrors ended, and I made a wonderful new mentor and friend!

Sometimes finding a mentor is as simple as asking for specific, tangible help. It may mean allowing other people to see our messes, but how else will they know we need mentoring?

A Mentor Shares—*Cheryl Ricker*

After our honeymoon, Dwight drove us from Canada to an apartment near his new job in Washington state, where I knew no one. Pregnant a few months later, I was lonely for my Canadian family, so I attended a church Bible Study and joined a mentoring ministry the church started.

"I'm a Canadian too," said Ellen "but that's not why I asked them to match me with you. I felt drawn to you. It was a God thing." Ellen had never mentored anyone other than her three daughters, so we were both equally new at this. I told Ellen my insecurities; she didn't judge. She spoke truth with tenderness. "All young moms battle nervousness. Even old ones do."

When I became pregnant with baby number two, Ellen prayed with me and dished out regular advice, when wanted. My husband also benefited from Ellen, who suggested hiring a babysitter for date nights. "You need to keep your love alive." Ellen and her hubby invited us to their home, where we watched them interact with playfulness and respect. We had come from fractured homes and appreciated seeing what a good marriage looked like.

I never dreamed God would lead me away from my mentor mom, but Dwight accepted a job in Minnesota. As Ellen helped clean out cupboards, I struggled to say goodbye. "You'll make new friends," she assured.

When we settled into our new home, Dwight and I started a Bible study for young couples and their children. Rachel, a second-grader, was especially quiet. I reached out in love to mentor her. Rachel graduated from college last week and posted a picture of the two of us on Facebook: "This gal is pretty much my second mother." How had this even happened? All I did was love, blink, and watch God do the rest.

M&M's *from* the Bible Share

Hannah was lonely in her bareness. She was depressed and desperate, and even her husband didn't understand why she was so sad. Instead of indulging her loneliness, Hannah called out to God for help, and Eli the prophet listened and prayed for her much like a mentor: "I am a woman who is deeply troubled. I have not been drinking wine or beer; I was pouring out my soul to the LORD. Do not take your servant for a wicked woman; I have been praying here out of my great anguish and grief." Eli answered, "Go in peace, and may the God of Israel grant you what you have asked of him" (1 Sam. 1:15–17).

God will send a godly woman to mentor us through our lonely times if we ask him and make an effort to find her, and then like Cheryl in A Mentor Shares, God will open doors for us to mentor.

Let's Talk about It

1. Why is it so hard for lonely women to meet other women?
2. Why would a mentor need to set boundaries?
3. What are some practical ideas to share with a lonely mentee?
4. How might a mentee take the first step to find a mentor in a new church or town?

Tragedy

The heartbreak of a tragedy often happens suddenly and without warning, or it can be a long and drawn out time of endless pain. Christians feel heartbreak and pain just like everyone. We have God to comfort us, but it still hurts. We desperately need reassurance from someone who survived a crisis with her faith not only still intact, but stronger than before.

Mentor Tips ....

People's reactions to experiences are different and unique. Your role is to empathize, encourage, and embolden her to seek God, the only one who can make sense out of a seemingly senseless crisis.

Here are some things you should *not* say or do:

- "I know *just* how you feel." No, you don't.
- "God has a plan." He does, but this is a Christian cliché.
- "Everything happens for a reason." This can seem condescending and uncaring.
- Telling stories of others who have it worse—this makes light of her pain and circumstances.
- Making her seem like she's a bad Christian if she feels like her faith is being tested—pray she'll trust God and grow closer to him over time.
- Letting her slip into depression or suicidal thoughts—if you see warning signs, inform her family, pastor, or both.

Here are things you *should* say or do:

- "Things are terrible now, but someday you *will* have a powerful testimony."
- "Journaling or writing down your emotions and feelings, and even ranting to God, helps."

- Share your story if she asks, but only enough to let her know you relate to her pain. Focus on her right now.
- Be kind-hearted, compassionate, and understanding.
- Provide a shoulder to cry on and a listening ear.
- Find ways to remain a part of her life if she withdraws. Show up with dinner or a plant. Keep calling or texting, even when she doesn't answer. She knows you still care.
- Provide suggestions of what helped you, but don't be disappointed if she rejects your ideas.
- Sit quietly if she's not ready to talk.

Mentee Tips ....

Your mentor can't make things right in your world, and it may even seem annoying if she has overcome something causing you so much pain. Let her be a source of Christian love and encouragement, but not your sole refuge. Ask her questions about how to survive this pain. Let her pray for, and over, you. She has committed to mentoring you through a difficult time when you shouldn't be alone with your thoughts and emotions. Don't push her away.

If you don't have a mentor, ask your pastor or women's ministry director to arrange for you to meet with another woman who has experienced a similar tragedy or difficult time.

God's Perspective: Search the Scriptures Together
- God is with you—Matt. 28:20
- Call on God—Ps. 77:2
- God will restore your hope—Ps. 119:49–50
- God will restore your joy—Jer. 31:13–14

A Mentee Shares—*Heather Gillis*

I'm a mother, wife, and nurse, but my passion is writing, so when our young son died tragically, I journaled my emotions, pain, and grief. After two years, I felt God's prompting to share my writings to help other parents who had lost children. I was ready for the next healing step, but I needed guidance. God placed Judith Couchman in my life as a writing coach, cheerleader, and mentor to walk me through starting a blog and launching a book. I was in awe of the wealth of knowledge and information she taught me. I thank God for my mentors.

A Mentor Shares—*Heather Gillis*

Four years after our son passed away, I had the opportunity to mentor other women going through hard times. Previously, I never comprehended 2 Corinthians 1:4 (*The Message*), "He comes alongside us when we go through hard times, and before you know it, he brings us alongside someone else who is going through hard times so that we can be there for that person just as God was there for us." Going through our tragedy, God always sent someone to say just what I needed to hear, a note of encouragement, or a prayer when I felt defeated. Then God showed me the power of coming alongside someone going through what we had experienced. God taught me how to pour out his love to another hurting mother, and in the process, I began to heal.

Before our son died, I didn't feel called to reach out to others. Now I consider it an honor when women who have lost a child, or are going through a crisis, seek me for healing and restoration counsel. I share what helped get me through my storm and emerge from the darkness—the hope and promises God showed in our devastation. I never thought of myself as a mentor, but now I can't stop sharing how God turned our tragedy into our biggest blessing. As a

MENTORING FOR ALL SEASONS

mentor—even though under unfortunate circumstances
—I've formed relationships and connected with women I
wouldn't have met if I hadn't made myself available to comfort them.

M&M's *from* the Bible Share

The sisters Mary and Martha suffered a tragic loss in the death of their
brother Lazarus, who was also Jesus's good friend. The sisters sent for
Jesus to come and heal their brother, but by the time Jesus arrived,
Lazarus was dead and buried. The sisters were distraught and upset
because Jesus didn't arrive sooner. They were sure he could have saved
their brother. Even Jesus wept over the loss of his friend (John 11:35).

Then Jesus raised Lazarus from the dead, and many people witnessed this miracle and became believers (John 11). Allowing others to
see Jesus comforting us during hard times can be just the witness they
need to accept Jesus as their Lord and Savior. Other times, Jesus uses
our tragedy as a testimony of his love and faithfulness in all our trials.

Let's Talk about It

1. Why would someone push others away during a tragic or difficult time?
2. Why is it good for Christians to let others see us going through
hard times?
3. Share a story of how Jesus helped you survive a tragedy.
4. How can we make our mess our message?

Caregiving, Aging Parents, and the Sandwich Generation

Many women still have children at home when they enter into caregiving for their aging parents: women in this season have become
known as the "sandwich generation." They live continuously in the

tension between parenting their children and their parents. Those women often feel exhausted, overworked, and overwhelmed. They desperately need advice and encouragement from a mentor who can give them perspective and help them achieve balance in their life.

Others may be empty nesters when parents need assistance, which often doesn't make things any easier since they may have full-time careers and other obligations, and the parents may not live close. Many decisions require that family members agree on maintaining the dignity of parents loved so dearly.

Caregiving isn't limited to aging parents. It can strike during any season of life and at any age—a spouse, a child, a relative, a friend—anyone you care about who can't take care of themselves.

A mentor who has survived a similar circumstance can be the anchor to keep the mentee from drowning in work, exhaustion, heartbreak, frustration, helplessness, and sometimes desperation. The mentor offers hope and reassurance that the mentee is going to make it too.

Mentor Tips ....

Annetta Dellinger mentored Renee, a young wife and mother who became a caregiver for her husband, who had colon cancer. Annetta describes herself as being in the "encouragement season." She offers wise advice about how to mentor someone in the caregiving season:

- Be a source of encouragement.
- Pray for your mentee each time God brings her to mind.
- Hug her often.
- Ask how you can help with transporting kids, grocery shopping, or running errands.
- Send cheerful, and sometimes humorous, cards to her *and* to the person she's caring for.
- Help her laugh.

- Cry with her when she needs a good cry.
- Remind her to take care of herself.
- Help her find balance and recognize when she needs outside help.

Mentee Tips ....

Karen Boerger in the A Mentee Shares segment offers important considerations for caregivers and those dealing with aging parents:

1. Applaud your own courage in handling day-to-day challenges.
2. Maintain a strong faith in God and stay in his Word for hope, support, and encouragement, to hear and feel every hurt from your heart.
3. Care for yourself to ensure you can continue daily care for your loved ones.
4. Don't be afraid to ask for, and accept, help when offered.
5. Take one day at a time.
6. Communicate with others.
7. Find a mentor with experience in what you're going through.

God's Perspective: Search the Scriptures Together

- Respect the dignity of the elderly—Lev. 19:32
- Care for others as God cares for each of us—Ps. 8:3–5, 36:6; Isa. 46:4
- You can do this with God's help—Isa. 40:29

A Mentee Shares—*Karen Boerger*

My husband had severe depression, my mother had Alzheimer's, my stepmother had cancer, and I helped with long-distance caregiving for my aunt.

Growing up, I watched mother care for her parents: good mentoring lessons. Everything wasn't sweetness and light, but her love for them overcame any harsh words. Usually, the elderly lash out because of pain and loss of independence—they just want to be strong and useful again. I learned caregivers need patience and perseverance.

Trying to cope with my husband's depression, mood swings, and suicidal tendencies sapped my energy. Back in the 1970s, no one talked about depression. Once my church family knew the situation, some came forward to talk about their depression, which was so helpful. Talking with trusted friend and mentor Annetta, who also had caregiving seasons, was the biggest help. We sat on each other's couches sharing and listening to painful challenges, offering support during prayerful heart-to-hearts, and encouraging each other to survive one more day.

When I was hurting, she sent funny cards, surprised me with a loaf of homemade bread in my car after church, tucked Scripture texts inside pill bottles, or rolled and tied Scripture with red ribbon notes saying "Open one-a-day." I appreciate her support, love, and encouragement to this day. Annetta and I wrote a book together to mentor other caregivers, *JOY-spirations for Caregivers*.

A Mentor Shares—*Debbie V.*

Taking care of my mother was difficult, but I learned so much from the experience. I cared for her while she lived in her own home for two years, until it became too much to clean and shop for two households and she wasn't eating properly and becoming emaciated. After much prayer, my husband Jerry and I decided to move her in with us. We were working full-time in real estate and had to move our office into our home so I was available to care for Mom's daily needs.

We're premarital counselors at church, and when we talk about extended family, one question asks, "If your in-laws were to become disabled, what would you be willing to do to assist them?" When we went through premarital counseling during our engagement more than twenty-nine years ago, we distinctly remember the pastor asking us the same question. We were only thirty-six and our parents were in good health, so our immediate response was, "Whatever is necessary to care for them." We didn't understand then the seriousness of such a commitment.

We cared for Mom in our home for two-and-a-half years. Nothing prepares us to become our parent's parent—a learn-as-you-go, difficult process requiring lots of prayer and cooperation, one I would gladly and thankfully do again. Most of our premarital couples haven't thought about this scenario, so we mentor them from our experience.

Debbie V. now mentors caregivers.

My mother raised me to be a "pleaser." I won favor by making her happy, and I felt guilty if I didn't. While caring for her, she had to-do lists. When I completed a list, another one appeared. I could never do enough. I prayed, but I felt guilt-ridden.

When the guilt was almost unbearable, we attended a mid-week service at church. My heart heard God's truth regarding my mother for the first time: "What you're doing for your mother is pleasing to me. That's *all* that matters.

You'll never please her completely—just do your best to continue pleasing *me*." I was *so* relieved!

I now have friends going through the caregiving season with demanding mothers. What a joy to see the relief on these dear women's faces when I share what God spoke to me!

M&M's *from* the Bible Share

Ruth had been gleaning the fields, bringing home food, and caring for her aging mother-in-law Naomi when Ruth met and married Boaz. They then had a child. Ruth was in the sandwich season, taking care of Naomi while becoming a new wife and mom. Scripture tells us Ruth's love and caring for Naomi didn't wane:

> The women said to Naomi: "Praise be to the LORD, who this day has not left you without a guardian-redeemer. May he become famous throughout Israel! He will renew your life and sustain you in your old age. For your daughter-in-law, who loves you and who is better to you than seven sons, has given him birth." Then Naomi took the child in her arms and cared for him. (Ruth 4:14–16)

Let's Talk about It

1. How could a mentor help refresh a caregiving mentee?
2. Why is caregiving lonely?
3. Why is it a good idea to discuss caring for in-laws during premarital counseling?
4. What can happen to a marriage when the couple doesn't agree on how to care for aging parents?

CHAPTER FOURTEEN

MIDLIFE AND GRANDPARENTING SEASON

My kids have left home. I'm going through menopause. I've lost my identity. I don't know who I am anymore. I feel like I'm going crazy. . . .

—Lois

She is clothed with strength and dignity,
and she laughs without fear of the future.

—Proverbs 31:25 NLT

Midlife and Menopause

When I started the Woman to Woman Mentoring Ministry at Saddleback Church, an elderly woman said she felt the church let her down when she went through menopause. Someone in the church should have prepared her for the physical and emotional changes she would experience. Since I was a few years away from menopause, I made a mental note, because if this was so important to her, it must be a season that mentoring should address.

Then *I* went through menopause! I called everyone I knew that was my age to see if what I was experiencing was *normal*. I finally found a Christian book on menopause, which I later gave to another clueless menopausal friend. Menopause causes a dramatic shift in a woman's hormones, body, thinking, attitude, and libido . . . not to mention hot flashes and weight gain. I have a friend whose husband is attributing their separation and pending divorce to his wife's radical changes during menopause. Hence the dramatic label "The Change"! No man will completely understand menopause, because his body doesn't change in the same way.

When I ask women if they received mentoring through menopause and midlife, they say, "No, but what a great idea!" The only person who responded "Yes!" was my friend and fellow author and speaker Pam Farrel, who took the initiative to mentor women in their midlife season, but she had to search out mentors for her own aging process—mentors who didn't realize they were mentoring her.

Mentor Tips ....

It may happen gradually, or seem like overnight, but eventually *every* woman has the alarming epiphany of not recognizing the body staring back at her from the mirror. Help your mentee understand that no matter how many changes her body goes through, her identity is in Christ, who never changes. For her mental, physical, and spiritual well-being, she needs to feel useful at any age. So help her find a place to serve or get involved in her church or community, especially if she's a mother feeling useless and lonely as her kids start leaving home. (See the Empty Nest Mom season in Chapter Twelve.) God speaks directly to these midlife "older" women to mentor younger women coming up behind them (Titus 2:3:5). This is a perfect time to fulfill his command.

Encourage her to take good care of her body, get regular checkups, see the doctor when something doesn't seem right, and don't be afraid to ask a medical professional about personal and physical changes. Remind her God's love for the young and old is forever, just as our love for God and our children never changes. Here are a few normal changes to prepare her for (and maybe have a few chuckles about).

- Hair loss where you want hair (on your head and eyebrows) and hair growth you don't want (chin hairs and mustaches)
- So many gray hairs that you must stop pulling them out, or go bald
- New aches and pains, especially in joints

- Hormonal changes that can cause hot flashes and affect attitude, emotions, and sex drive
- The days seeming to fly by quicker than when younger
- Difficulty losing or maintaining weight
- Adjusting mentally and emotionally to being the "older" woman
- Not worrying so much about what others think (Use this newfound freedom wisely and constructively.)

For each of the changes your mentee is going to face, encourage her to take proactive steps where needed. Here are some tips to share with her:

- For aches and joint stiffness, it will help to stay active when possible: walk, swim, bike, or join a gym class.
- Discuss hormonal changes with your doctor.
- Since it might be more difficult to maintain or lose weight, modify your diet and increase exercise.
- Laugh more and don't take yourself so seriously.
- Aging is a gift from God, so rejoice you're still alive. It's a blessing being the Titus 2 "older" woman with many life experiences to share with a younger woman.
- Ask God how he wants to use you in this season.

Mentee Tips ....

Find a mentor who is enjoying, or enjoyed, her midlife season. It's easy to find someone to commiserate with, but you want inspiration to live life to the fullest, not simply endure. God has you here for a reason, so seek his will and purpose in every season. Share how you feel about your physical and emotional changes, but remember that the purpose of having a mentor is to help you *prevail*, not *ail*, so listen to her wise experience and advice and put them into practice.

God's Perspective: Search the Scriptures Together

- Maintain your joy at any age—Prov. 31:25
- Life is full of change—Eccles. 3:1–8

A Mentee Shares—*Pam Farrel*

In my early forties, I was a women's ministry director for the church my husband Bill pastored. I noticed women in their midlife years, ages thirty-eight through fifty-eight, were in the press of life—dealing with tweens/teens, college kids, and possibly becoming grandparents—while navigating the landmines of kids' dating, driving, and avoiding drinking and drugs. Add the financial strain of cars, proms, prodigals, graduations, college tuitions, and weddings.

Or a woman with a "bonus baby" after forty who has a teething toddler while incurring hot flashes and hormone changes. It also could be a season of marital strife when a midlife husband suddenly wants to sell the family van and buy a Harley motorcycle or red convertible and ride off into the stress-free sunset.

Statistically, this is the season of life with the highest divorce rate. Typical marital challenges are affairs, addictions, or a spouse who wants to abandon responsibilities. The couple might have health issues, while caring for aging parents as well! On the upside, careers could be peaking and children might be launching their own lives.

I told Bill *we* were in our peak: "Our life is like a hand-crocheted afghan. Our teen kids are tracking with God. You grew our church and moved our congregation into a beautiful new building. I love my roles as women's ministry director, wife, mom, and Christian speaker. We've written thirty books, with one on the Christian bestseller list! Life doesn't get much better than this!"

Then the midlife express rolled into our happy life, and it was as if someone grabbed one string of our life afghan and unraveled our life. We were on a media tour for *Men Are Like Waffles, Women Are Like Spaghetti* when Bill started feeling ill. The diagnosis, erratic high blood pressure, got our attention because his father and grandfather had strokes in their forties. Bill's physician said, "You're burning the candle at both ends: full-time pastor *and* writer/speaker."

Bill resigned the senior pastor position of fifteen years. My empty-nest emotions accompanied this season of tremendous adjustment as we launched our first son into college. Then my forty-year-old brother survived a heart attack, reminding *me* of heart health, since our father had a fatal heart attack.

A Mentor Shares—*Pam Farrel*

As I watched midlife season maladies occurring in my life and those around me, I rallied a group of friends in life's second half who wanted "the rest of life to be the best of life." We created Seasoned Sisters, and for a decade I became a researcher bringing wisdom, comfort, and answers to our varied midlife questions. I wrote *10 Secrets of Living Smart, Savvy, and Strong* because I had a heart to mentor women through midlife challenges. Seasoned Sisters groups sprung up around the world, and our local group grew. We were committed to a pattern of trusting, praying, laughing, learning, celebrating, encouraging, and supporting each other.

M&M's *from* the Bible Share

God chose two older women to have surprise babies: Sarah, the mother of Isaac, and Elizabeth, the mother of John the Baptist. These women's bodies were well beyond menopause, so what a shock this was to them and their husbands! We can see why Abraham and Sarah laughed: "Abraham fell facedown; he laughed and said to himself, 'Will a son be born to a man a hundred years old? Will Sarah bear a child at the age of ninety?'" (Gen. 17:17). "Sarah laughed to herself as she thought, 'After I am worn out and my lord is old, will I now have this pleasure?'" (Gen. 18:12). Zechariah, Elizabeth's husband, questioned this possibility: "Zechariah asked the angel, 'How can I be sure of this? I am an old man and my wife is well along in years'" (Luke 1:18).

Perhaps God wants us to see we're never too old for him to use us for his purposes: to birth new spiritual life in the baby Christians and younger women he puts before us to mentor.

Let's Talk about It

1. Why don't women typically mentor each other through midlife?
2. How would the menopause season be easier if older women mentored women coming up behind them?
3. Is this a new concept to you—older women being mentored by even older women?
4. How could a menopausal woman's changes wreak havoc in her marriage?

Grandparenting

When I became a grandparent for the first time, I felt like God saved the best season for last. As someone once said, being a mother is the most important job in the world, but being a grandmother is the most fun! I love being Grammie to our eleven grandchildren.

Mothering is a season filled with enormous responsibility and requiring vast amounts of energy, time, and focus. Grandparenting is a season of reaping the benefits and rewards of the parenting season—more leisurely time to play with and enjoy the grandchildren. Dr. Roman Hanks wrote an insightful article titled "Connecting the Generations: The New Role of Grandparents":

> It is my belief that grandparenting is the most important family role of the new [twenty-first] century. I say that because grandparents are just now discovering all the possibilities of relating to their grandchildren. Whether they are providing full-time care or working on a deeply supportive relationship, grandparents will have influence over a longer period of their grandchildren's lives than ever before. They will be healthier, more active, more involved, and more purposeful in relating to their grandchildren than were the grandparents that you and I knew. Their influence will spread beyond their own families.[1]

Of course, some grandparents like Lisa B. are raising their grandchildren; some are helping mom with daycare while she works or assisting with homeschooling; others don't live near their grandchildren. Thankfully, technology makes it possible to stay in touch and even have face-to-face contact with video calls.

Not every child enjoys the privilege of having grandparents, so those of us who are still alive should consider being a grandparent an honor and gift from the Lord.

Mentor Tips ....

Grandparenting can be lots of fun, but it's also challenging. Listen to what your mentee is experiencing; if she has problems, be careful not to tout or brag about what a great relationship you have with your grandkids and their parents. She might make comparisons and feel badly because you have what she desires. Or perhaps she's struggling with this season because it marks the inevitable aging process.

Sometimes friction with the parents interferes with the hoped-for relationship with grandchildren. She can still pray for the family, show unconditional love, and attempt to resolve the issues (Heb. 12:14). It may mean humbling herself and asking for forgiveness, even when she doesn't think she's at fault. Remind her that replacing pride and animosity with love and kindness is so worth the opportunity to spend precious time with her grandchildren.

Find ways to help her enjoy being a grandmother, whatever her circumstances. Help her remember that her grandchildren carry on her legacy and traditions, and she wants to be a sweet memory to them. Here are some suggested questions to discuss together:

- What do your children expect of you as a grandparent?
- How much involvement do you want in babysitting the grandkids? How available do you want to be?
- How can you support your children's parenting roles and rules?
- How often will you visit and for how long?
- Do the parents welcome your suggestions and wisdom? Should you wait for them to ask before offering an opinion?
- Can you give the grandchildren gifts? What foods? Any recreation or toy restrictions?
- Will you be allowed to discipline the grandchildren?
- How will you celebrate holidays?
- Will they allow you to share Jesus with the grandchildren?
- If a blended family, how will you grandparent your step-children's children?

Mentee Tips ....

Grandparenting can be a blessed and joyous experience, or one of confusion, disappointment, and frustration. Share with your mentor the joys and struggles of your grandparenting season. Allow her to be a source of encouragement with tips of what helped her adjust to being a grandmother. She can help you set realistic grandma expectations and give good advice on how not to take too personally some of the responses of your children and grandchildren.

God's Perspective: Search the Scriptures Together

- God blesses us as grandparents—Prov. 17:6
- Tell your grandchildren about God—Deut. 4:9
- Pray for your grandchildren to honor God; set a godly example—Deut. 6:1–2
- Enjoy your grandchildren—Ps. 128:6

A Mentee Shares—*Lisa B.*

It hasn't been easy raising my granddaughter since birth. During the teen years it was especially hard to be a parent instead of enjoying the grandparenting season. I don't have support from family or a close friend—but there *is* one woman in church I truly believe prays for us.

A Mentor Shares—*Lillian Penner*

I was mentoring a friend when she became a grandmother for the first time. She experienced challenges with her son and his wife similar to what I also had experienced.

Her son's in-laws live in the same area, and his wife is close to her family. My mentee felt left out because the couple spent more time with the wife's family. I suggested she pray and ask God for wisdom in how to respond when she had the opportunity, and with time, the situation would change. My friend slowly found her place in their family and is now enjoying her three grandchildren.

Grandparents need to remember what a big adjustment it is becoming new parents. As excited as we are to have grandchildren, sometimes we have to wait to see where the parents feel comfortable in fitting us into their family circle.

M&M's *from* the Bible Share

Lois, the grandmother of Timothy, has the distinction of being the only grandmother actually named as a grandmother in the Bible. Paul wrote about Lois, "I am reminded of your sincere faith, which first lived in your grandmother Lois and in your mother Eunice and, I am persuaded, now lives in you also" (2 Tim. 1:5). A legacy every grandmother should leave in her grandchildren.

Let's Talk about It

1. What is the best thing and the worst thing about being a grandmother?
2. What was your reaction when you learned you would be a grandmother for the first time?
3. How did you arrive at the name your grandchildren would call you?
4. How would you describe your relationship with your grandchildren?

CHAPTER FIFTEEN

RETIRING, DOWNSIZING, AND SENIOR SEASON

Our senior years should be the best years of our life!
—Penelope Carlevato

Wisdom belongs to the aged, and understanding to the old.
—Job 12:12 NLT

As we approach our senior season, we look forward to retiring, which often means downsizing our home and possessions. Sometimes downsizing starts first as the kids leave the nest and you don't need the responsibilities and financial burden of a large house and your body is ready for a rest from the upkeep required. In retirement years, you want freedom to travel or pursue other interests outside the home. Often this might mean moving to be closer to grandkids, aging parents, or your dream retirement spot.

Retiring and downsizing can play emotional havoc as you fluctuate between feelings of *adventure* and *anxiety*. If work has been a main source of identity and purpose, this is the opportunity to develop new interests and motivations that further God's kingdom work.

Downsizing is nostalgic . . . reflecting on all the mementoes and pictures of past years can lead to a sense of loss and sadness. A mentor who has weathered this season and found the joy and freedom of owning less and working less in her senior years can help a mentee decide what to keep from the past and what to let go of for the future.

Mentor Tips

Discuss with your mentee that even when we retire from doing work providing *earthly riches*, we never retire from doing God's work providing *eternal riches* (Eph. 3:8). Whether in a season of retiring, downsizing, or just preparing to enjoy senior years, help her assess her abilities and gifts and start making plans for how God can use her time and resources to further his earthly kingdom. Focus on discovering her purpose in this season by using her God-given gifts to share the gospel for his glory. Married couples should consider how to enjoy ministering together in this season. If your mentee is spiritually ready, encourage her to become a mentor. She has many life experiences to share and more free time to do it!

Mentee Tips

In downsizing, you might have questions to ask your mentor, similar to those of Pam Farrel in the A Mentee Shares section:

- How do you decide what to keep, toss, give away, or sell?
- How do you handle nostalgia and sadness of selling the "family home"?
- How do you care for your own health while possibly caring for elderly family members?
- How do you cope with financial pressures?
- What if you want to start a new business or ministry at the age most retire?
- How do you maintain stamina when your body might be screaming for a nap?
- What should you do to nurture your marriage during the plethora of life's pressures?
- How do you hold onto God when life is a whirlwind of emotions, responsibilities, and unpredictability?

- What can you do to remain a positive role model for family, mentees, and others when you feel like curling up in bed with a half gallon of ice cream.

God's Perspective: Search the Scriptures Together
- You have more time to tell others about Jesus—Acts 20:24
- Downsizing allows you to focus on what has kingdom value; you're not taking anything when you leave this world, so do your giving while you're living—Ps. 49:16; Matt. 19:21; 1 Tim. 6:7
- You've earned enough; relax, enjoy, and serve God— Prov. 27:24; Ps. 62:5, 90:17; Phil. 4:18–20
- Jesus said don't be greedy—Luke 12:15

A Mentee Shares—*Pam Farrel*

Pam Farrel is not yet in the senior season and still is in full-time ministry with her husband, but she's preparing by downsizing and seeking wise counsel from older mentors.

> Life stabilized some for Bill and me after he retired from pastoring a church [see A Mentee Shares and A Mentor Shares in the Midlife and Menopause season of Chapter 14]. God poured joy back into our lives as our three sons married and gave us precious grandchildren. Bill landed a ministry position he loved, and God continued to bless our writing and speaking ministry.
>
> During my forties, I regularly sought out good friend Carole Lewis, who layered wisdom and courage into my life. Carole had survived many life challenges: bankruptcy, being a caregiver to her late husband, her daughter's death by a drunk driver, and a hurricane leveling her seaside home. When Carole turned seventy, she gathered a group

and shared the truth about "getting old," and we learned even more of the insider info of how to age gracefully. I felt confident to navigate any upcoming changes—until, as Bill and I entered our fifties, I had my first health scare, and facing down death altered my optimistic view of the future.

Our three sons settled with their families outside of California where we live, and Bill was tired of caring for our property, so we began praying about downsizing. We would work a slow, methodical plan of sorting, cleaning, selling, and giving away a lifetime of possessions over the next few years. A gradual transition seemed doable. Then Bill's eighty-seven-year-old parents, who live a ten-hour round trip drive away, began needing him more, cutting into his worktime. I felt pressure to do the work Bill typically handled in our ministry and business. Our personal finances suffered. Exhaustion and stress made us acutely aware of the need to care for our own health.

We had to sell and move quickly. I wasn't a happy camper. Now the downsizing and move were *completely* out of my control. I was depressed, stressed, and angry. I worried about Bill and his folks but felt I couldn't express my emotions. I knew caring for my in-laws was the right thing to do, but a history of family dysfunctions made this the hardest ministry God ever asked of us. The sheer amount of work to prepare our home for sale in a competitive, still recovering, housing market was overwhelming. Our own previous health scares warned us we couldn't just work harder and pull all-nighters like in our younger days.

Moving away from our deep, loyal, supportive friends, and further away from our children and grandchildren, left me depressed and hopeless. I needed some serious mentoring by women who had experienced similar trauma and somehow lived to tell about it! I needed godly counsel.

I had a speaking engagement in the hometown of Carole Lewis, and another speaker/author friend about a decade older than me, Karen Porter. I messaged my friends, asking if we could meet for dinner. Amazing how much mentoring can happen over a few hours when the recipient is desperate for help! A teachable heart is like a sponge soaking up wisdom. I had so many questions.

I needed the experienced, valid, expert advice, insight, and wisdom from women who had been there, and not just *survived* but *thrived* through the storm. These women were polished diamonds—gems of God—glorifying Christ with their overcomer attitudes. I wanted to become like them, radiating Jesus no matter what curve balls life was throwing my way.

A Mentor Shares—*Karen Porter*

I didn't feel I was formally mentoring Pam Farrel, but I'm a listening friend. She is busy and "on stage" most of the time, so to have a quiet conversation is a treat for her. Especially since I don't talk as much as I listen. As she and Bill have made transitions from full-time church ministry to full-time speaking ministry, and now as they downsize so they can live near and care for his parents, I have advice about living in a new way. Downsizing from a big house to a small one is a deliberate and difficult task. But the result is freedom—in living and enjoying life. I've downsized five times . . . at first not by choice, but now because it's life changing.

Going from a guaranteed salary to depending on God for income is an adventure in trust. You never know where money is coming from, but you learn to know God will provide—because that's what he does. When I lost my corporate job to a foreign company takeover, we lost everything—but I wouldn't go back for triple the salary now. God is too good at providing. No matter what you need, He always shows up.

I think being a mentor to Pam really only means I'm on the road a bit ahead of her. I've seen the curves and hazards and the joy of the view—so I tell her about it. It's a sweet friendship/mentorship.

M&M's *from* the Bible Share

Priscilla and Aquila must have traveled light; they had a tent-making business and were missionaries traveling with Paul. When Paul picked up and went to another place, they went with him, set up home and business, and opened their home as a house church. They couldn't have taken much with them—just the essentials for life, business, and ministry. We don't have a record of their ever retiring.

Let's Talk about It

1. Why is it so hard to let go of lifelong possessions?
2. How do you decide what to keep when downsizing?
3. Do you have a retirement plan?
4. What ministry will you serve in after retiring?

CHAPTER SIXTEEN

AGING AND DYING SEASON

*I come from a big Christian family and
we just mentor each other as we grow older.*

—Bette

*Do not cast me away when I am old;
do not forsake me when my strength is gone. . . .
Even when I am old and gray,
do not forsake me, my God,
till I declare your power to the next generation,
your mighty acts to all who are to come.*

—Psalm 71:9, 18

A time to be born and a time to die.

—Ecclesiastes 3:1

As I sought mentoring stories on aging, I was surprised so few women mentored each other during this twilight season. They were often willing to mentor younger women, but didn't think they needed mentoring as they matured. We can *always* learn from each other at any age.

Dying is a hard season to write about—or even think about—but one we *all* face. Death doesn't always wait until we're older either. Many seniors watch younger loved ones die first—they grieve and ache for a life over far too soon.

Other times, the death season delays until after a long, full life, yet we still find it hard to let go of our loved ones . . . and even harder for them to let go of us. Photographer Gaia Squarci chronicled in photos the most memorable moments of the five months she spent in Italy with "Nonna Dida," her grandmother, as Nonna was dying. "In the moments we shared I had the chance to witness her keep all her dignity while letting go of the pride, confronting a fast-changing body without any shyness, and without ever losing her femininity."[1]

Until we take our last breath, God can use us to mentor others in how to age with grace and die well. I hope you see God isn't done with you yet and that he wants you to be a witness for him until he takes you home to heaven. As Christians, we never age out of doing kingdom work.

Mentor Tips ....

If you're in the aging season yourself, your mentee may have many questions about how to navigate body changes and physical limitations. Share as openly as you feel comfortable.

If your mentee is a Christian who is housebound, in a nursing or retirement home, or not easily mobile, remind her she can still be a mentor and mentees could come to her. Or women already around her could benefit from her years of experiences walking with the Lord. Or if she's adept at electronics, she can share devotionals on social media or even face-to-face on Skype.

If she's not a believer and is dying, God may use you to be her last chance to spend eternity in heaven. Try to find out what's holding her back from making a commitment. Read her the book, or watch the movie, *The Case for Christ*. Or watch the movie *God's Not Dead* with her, and pray her heart softens before it stops beating.

If your mentee isn't aged or dying herself, but is dealing with someone at the end of his or her life, Annetta Dillinger has wise mentoring advice: as she told her friend Patty, dying from breast cancer, "I will walk with you." Annetta watched her dear friend take her last breath on earth. As a mentor, consider Annetta's wisdom and/or pass on her suggestions to your mentee:

- It's okay to cry. Get small tissue packages with fun sayings or pictures on them. Keep a package for yourself and give some to her. Jesus cried. We can too.
- Say what's on your heart, even the hard things. I regret I didn't.
- Ask about things she wants you to do for her, her family, organizations, etc. If she can dictate thoughts, write them down and give to her family.
- Just be there for her. Smile. Hold her hand. Rub lotion on her arms. Bring humor.
- Get matching water cups or coffee/tea mugs for you and her. Talk about things you've done together. Have a positive joy-filled spirit. She knows your heart is breaking, without you saying a word.
- Thank her for what she helped you do or did for you. Pour out your heart and hurt. This is true heart-connection time.
- Read her a Psalm or prayer.
- Talk to her about heaven: the joy of salvation. We talked about the angels celebrating as she walked into heaven.
- · Hug, cry, and just be with her as the Holy Spirit guides.
- Ask important questions the family won't think of at the time: computer passwords, where special things are kept, important dates, promises made, and so on.
- Frame a picture of the two of you taken before she became ill. Keep it near her bedside, and later in your home.
- Continue to talk about her memories to the family. She may be out of sight, but she is never out of mind.

The most important thing to share with a mentee who has someone close to them dying is to be positive the dying person knows Jesus as his or her Savior. Even if they accept him with their dying breath, they will spend eternity with you and your mentee in heaven. Help your mentee find the right time and summon the courage to have that discussion. She has nothing to lose, but the dying person has eternity at stake. (The Appendix has a Seeker Question and a Salvation Prayer.)

Mentee Tips ....

You can learn so much from an elderly person or relative and perhaps be their eyes and ears. Heather B. says, "I've been inspired to read Scripture to my grandparents. I live in Florida; they live in Indiana. In their eighties, it's hard to read their Bible. Every Friday at 4:00 pm, I call them. We encourage each other and learn from each other." If someone close to you is aging or dying, and you need wise counsel, a mentor who has experienced this season can answer your questions and offer support. If the person doesn't know Jesus as their Savior, ask your mentor to help you have the courage to share the Gospel with them.

If you're in the aging season, find a mentor who is a little further along in this season who will answer your questions about how to make the most of every day the Lord gives you of life.

If you know you'll soon be with Jesus, a godly mentor can help you use these last days for God's glory. She can be your hands and feet to write thoughts you want to leave behind; but most importantly, your mentor will pray and talk with you as God brings you closer to home.

The most valuable legacy to leave your loved ones who know Jesus as their Savior is the assurance you are going home to be with Jesus, and you will see them again. If a friend or family member doesn't know Jesus, maybe this is the time he or she will be open to hearing about salvation from you with your last few breaths. God will use you until the very end.

God's Perspective: Search the Scriptures Together
- Aging is a beautiful thing—Prov. 16:31, 20:29
- God loves and cares for the elderly—Ps. 71:5; Isa. 46:4

- Eternal life awaits those who believe in Jesus Christ as their Lord and Savior—Ps. 56:13, 68:20; John 3:16, 17:3; Rom. 6:23
- Knowing that we have to die to be with Jesus can bring us peace as we age and when a loved one who knows Jesus as their Savior dies; nearing death can also motivate us to make sure a loved one has every opportunity to become a believer—1 Cor. 15:53–58

A Mentee Shares—*Poppy Smith*

I was born in England and grew up there and in Sri Lanka, Singapore, and Kenya. At age seventeen, I went to live in Nairobi and attended a little English church, where an older woman took me under her wing for the next five years until I married my American husband and came to America. That's when my mentor's role became much more crucial in my life. She and her husband went back to England, and I would pour out my anger and pain in letters to her about how painful and overwhelming it was adjusting to a new marriage and country, where I had no family or friends.

She wrote back, constantly pointing me to God's love and purposes in my life through trials.

I recently visited my nearly ninety-year-old English mentor in England—a profound influence on me for decades as she counseled me in letters. Still sharp, mentally and spiritually, she now sends emails

She recently said when she shared Scriptures she was also applying them to her heart and painful circumstances that drove her deeper in the Lord. Mentoring and influencing another doesn't have to wait until your own life is smooth and pain free. I've told her God put her in my life at the beginning of my walk with him because he knew the struggles I'd have—which she knew personally, yet she clung to him. I owe her my marriage, my ministry, and who I've become by God's grace. In her, God gave me a gift of love and ministry.

A Mentor Shares—*Poppy Smith*

In the Introduction, I told the story of reading Lucibel Van Atta's book *Women Encouraging Women*. Twenty years later, I discovered that Lucibel, "Lucki," was a mentor of my author friend Poppy Smith. Poppy had the privilege of spending time with Lucki in her last days.

I was guest teaching for a church's women's ministry group. Lucki attended with one of her mentees. After a couple of weeks, she approached me and asked, "Have you written what you're teaching?" I said, "No." She invited me to her writing critique group and told me about the Oregon Christian Writers summer conference, and I went on to become a published author and speaker!

I visited Lucki about a month before she passed away. She knew she was dying from kidney failure and diabetes, but she was comfortable talking about this season of life. What an amazing opportunity to spend time with someone facing death unafraid, at peace, and living in Christ to the end.

The older women I know would never think of themselves as my "mentors"—just as women sharing the reality of their walk with Jesus—but their influence fuels my desire to do the same now that I'm the "older woman," whether speaking, writing, leading a group, or encouraging, listening, praying, or biblically counseling individually. I'm watching in amazement as God keeps adding young thirtyish women to my home mentoring group. They're so alive and they love coming!

M&M's *from* the Bible Share

When Mary and Joseph took baby Jesus to the temple in Jerusalem, they encountered Anna, a prophetess who continued her evangelism ministry about the Messiah, even as an old woman:

> When the time came for the purification rites required by the Law of Moses, Joseph and Mary took him to Jerusalem to present him to the Lord .... There was also a prophet, Anna, the daughter of Penuel, of the tribe of Asher. She was very old; she had lived with her husband seven years after her marriage, and then was a widow until she was eighty-four. She never left the temple but worshiped night and day, fasting and praying. Coming up to them at that very moment, she gave thanks to God and spoke about the child to all who were looking forward to the redemption of Jerusalem. (Luke 2:22, 36–38)

Let's Talk about It

1. What is the scariest part about growing older?
2. Why do people try so hard to remain young?
3. If you were to die tonight, are you ready to be with Jesus?
4. Who do you know who doesn't have the assurance of eternal life? How does God want you to start that conversation?

EPILOGUE

Some women have had the same mentor throughout all their life seasons. When I read the story "JoAnn Leavell: My Mentor and Me" by my dear friend Dr. Rhonda Kelley, I knew I had to ask Rhonda for permission to share parts of it with you. Enjoy this illustration of how the M&M relationship of Rhonda Kelley and the late JoAnn Leavell reflects the heart of *Mentoring for All Seasons*.

> JoAnn Leavell has been an important part of my life for 39 years! As a young bride, I quickly connected with Mrs. Leavell: we were both from New Orleans, lived on campus with our husbands at NOBTS [New Orleans Baptist Theological Seminary], went to First Baptist New Orleans, and loved to talk! I was in her first student wives class at NOBTS, and she became a beloved mentor and friend.
>
> *As a student wife*, Mrs. Leavell taught me important truths:
>
> 1. You never have a second chance to make a first impression.
> 2. Learn to say "no" with your teeth showing (a smile).
> 3. You don't have to do everything in the church, but you do have to do something.

4. The bigger the earrings, the better.

5. Learn to cry pretty. (I still struggle with this, especially saying good-bye to my friend and mentor.)

While working on his doctorate, my husband Chuck worked as a grader for Dr. Leavell [Mrs. Leavell's husband]. Dr. Leavell offered Chuck a position teaching evangelism at NOBTS, and Chuck accepted. Our ministry connection with the Leavells continued during Chuck's thirteen years on faculty, and Dr. Leavell became president of NOBTS.

As a professor's wife, Mrs. Leavell trained me for ministry and shared life lessons along the way:

1. If you love me, call me JoAnn. That was hard! She was Mrs. Leavell and held my greatest respect.

2. If you're sick on Sunday morning, move your car from the driveway so the students won't think you're sleeping in.

3. If you don't pick up the trash on campus, no one will.

4. A written thank you note is a lasting ministry.

5. Wear black; it looks better on your hips.

During those years, I had the joy of working with JoAnn on many campus events, and we planned two "big women's conferences." One of her personal passions was the JoAnn Leavell Clothing Ministry. It was my joy to accompany her to Stein Mart to dress many grateful student wives. On occasion, she would fling open the door of the dressing room to examine an outfit and exclaim, "Honey, that color doesn't work for you." The student wives were always grateful for her generosity and personal attention. We continue this ministry in her memory.

JoAnn wrote two books; her "Alpha and Omega!" *Joy in the Journey* was a reflection on life after her "episode" (a stroke). I had the joy of writing *Don't Miss the Blessing* with her. Dr. Leavell said I was "the only person who could outline JoAnn!" We revised the book for ministry wives in 2010. She spent a week at the Leavell's apartment on campus, and we worked through the manuscript while drinking coffee and reminiscing. I read aloud each word of the book for her to approve or reject, as she often digressed to tell the rest of the story—a special time of bonding.

In March 1996, my husband assumed the office of president of NOBTS, succeeding JoAnn's husband.

As the president's wife, Mrs. Leavell encouraged me and offered wise counsel:

1. Never put your photo on the cover of the seminary cookbook.
2. Always keep the downstairs ready for company.
3. Students come and go, but you can still make a lasting difference in their lives.
4. Don't try to be me. Be better . . . be yourself!
5. People will give you lots of advice. Let it go in one ear and out the other. Listen to God!

What a privilege to continue the Ministry Wife Program, Women's Auxiliary, and the Clothing Ministry loved so dearly by JoAnn Leavell. She was a bigger-than-life personality who had a profound impact on my life. I miss her every day and always thank God for my mentor![1]

APPENDIX

Choosing a Mentor

An excerpt from *And It Was Beautiful* by the late Kara Tippetts

Apart from the Holy Spirit, it has been the mentors in my life who have made the longest-lasting, deepest impact on who I am as a person. Some mentors were women I specifically asked to mentor me. Some were women who opened their lives wide open for me to watch. But both nurtured new strength in me. Here are a few things that have served me well in finding a mentor.

First, do they love their family well and speak with love and admiration of their husbands? Can these be areas of tension and struggle in a family? Yes, but I look to see if their overall desire is to move toward a spouse and children, and not away.

Second, do they speak vulnerably about weakness, or are they more concerned about appearances? I have found this area to be critical. I struggle to share openly with someone who wants to appear they have it all figured out. I look to see if they are willing to speak openly about where God is challenging them, and are open about themselves without bashing others.

Third, and most important, do they seek Jesus in their moments throughout the day, especially the mundane? Do they see their neediness and weakness, and are they able to be wrong and be corrected by Scripture?

When Jason [my husband] was a youth director, we had the privilege of seeing kids who truly loved Jesus. From that observation, we often sought out their parents. We wanted to sit at their feet, eat at their table, and watch how they did it. I love to watch someone discipline with kindness. I love to watch someone including their children in the events of the home. I love watching someone loving their spouse creatively. And I really love to see women involved in community building. You can receive a lot of mentoring just by watching.

Common interests help as well. I have had mamas show me a craft, women who love to write as well as read, ladies who love to garden, build a fire, and cook, and women who just cannot get enough of their Bibles. I often try to enter the life of a person who might be a good fit as a mentor in a place of common joy. I want my mentors to be my friends, as I want to befriend the women I mentor.

Things to be wary of? Be careful of people who like to gossip. Be willing to be flexible. Mentoring relationships take on so many different looks. Sitting down across from one another with Bibles open every week? That's an awesome model, but it's certainly not the only one. Look for someone who will promote freedom in Christ, not tie you up in a load of legalism.

Finally, as you search for a safe place, be a safe place in return. God loves seeing us seeking Him together.[1]

Mentor-Seeking Checklist

When seeking a mentor or spiritual mother, look at her life and relationships. Ask yourself these questions before approaching someone to be your mentor.

- ☑ Is she a godly woman inside and outside her home?
- ☑ If married, does she have a loving relationship with her husband, and is he a godly man? Do they study God's Word and pray together?
- ☑ How does she handle life's difficulties?
- ☑ Do you admire her and the way she lives her life?
- ☑ Would you characterize her as a righteous woman?
- ☑ Is she leading a life you would like for yourself?
- ☑ Is she the woman today you want to become?
- ☑ Does she love Jesus, and does she show it?

Remember, even if she says no when you ask her, don't let that stop you from asking someone else. She wasn't the mentor for you this season.

Realistic Expectations for Your Mentor

- She isn't perfect and knowledgeable in *every* area of life or the Bible. Understand she's human and has weaknesses.
- A friendship may develop that lasts over a lifetime, but usually mentoring relationships are for a season.
- You're not obligated to follow her every suggestion and idea. Pray and let the Holy Spirit guide you, but weigh carefully whether she might be right.
- Beware of a mentor who validates everything you do and say; find one who challenges you to be a better person.
- She should *always* call a sin a sin—and provide you a biblical perspective.
- Her focus should be on growing *with* you to be more Christlike in every area and season of both your lives.

Advantages of Having a Mentor

Julie Morris, author of *Guided by Him . . . To a Thinner, Not So Stressed-Out You*, learned the following while mentoring over the last thirty-five years, and I've added a few things I learned too!

Benefits for Mentees

- You will be more aware of your actions when you know a mentor will ask.
- You will be encouraged to accomplish goals with accountability and responsibility.
- You have someone to call when you need prayer, understanding, or encouragement.
- You have a friend who knows you—warts and all—and accepts, affirms, reassures, and challenges you to try new things.
- You can learn from your mentor's mistakes, benefit from her experiences, and grow because of her confidence that God is at work in you.

Characteristics of Mentors

- They don't wear masks or pretend perfection, but admit mistakes and challenges.
- They don't feel the responsibility to *make* you do the right thing, and they don't get angry when you don't.
- They don't give unrequested advice or heap on guilt.
- They don't judge or give lectures.
- They don't let you make excuses or pretend you're doing okay when you're not.
- They aren't codependent—feeling good if you do well and bad if you don't.
- They'll stop your pity party, so you can focus on ways to solve your problems with God's help.

- They won't let you dump your problems on them.
- They will be your cheerleader, not police you.
- They make time to listen.
- They never talk behind your back or tell others what you share.
- They are trustworthy.
- They ask thought-provoking questions, such as "How could you have made a better choice?"
- They know their job is to pray for you, encourage you, and point you to the only One who can change you.
- They help change your attitude about your mistakes and weaknesses. They rejoice in God's sufficiency to work in and through you.

Should You Mentor?

Your role as a mentor is to facilitate, educate, commemorate, celebrate, and guide your mentee to a deeper relationship with Christ and show her ways to apply the Bible to her life. But not *every* mentee is a good match for you and your experiences. Sometimes after prayer and evaluation, you might need to decline a mentoring request. In "Who—Me? She's Asking Me to Mentor Her," Karen Trigg[2] offers points to consider before agreeing to mentor someone, and I've added a few to think about too:

1. Ask the potential mentee, "What do you want from a mentoring relationship?" This helps clarify her reasons and motivation for wanting you to mentor her. She may just want to get close to you.

2. As she answers, *listen well;* ask specific questions in natural conversation to help her focus on her goals for the relationship.

- Are you seeking accountability? If so, in what areas?
- Do you want to do a Bible study? Read a book? What topic?

- Do you want to spend time together in Q&A and discussions?
- How often were you hoping to meet?
- Are you willing to let me be intentional and ask hard questions?
- Will you be open with me, knowing I have your best interest at heart?

3. Pray about her answers before agreeing. As you consider whether to mentor her, ask yourself:

- What time do *I* have to offer? What fits best in *my* schedule?
- How often is best for me to meet and where? My home? A coffee shop or bookstore?
- Can I put my family's needs before her needs?
- Am *I* willing to ask hard questions?
- Do I have experience in her life season? If not, do I feel comfortable mentoring her?
- Is she looking for something more than mentoring?

If you prayerfully agree to mentor her, start with three to six months, and then reevaluate if you both want to continue. If you prayerfully decide not to mentor her, or this isn't a good time, encourage her to keep seeking a mentor.

What Should M&M's Do When They Meet?

Based on the season your mentee is in and the goals you decide for the relationship, you may do a Bible study, read a book, or simply spend time in prayer and discussion. Let the Holy Spirit guide your time together; every M&M relationship is unique. Here are a few guidelines for each meeting:

1. *Always start and close your time together in prayer.* If your mentee isn't comfortable praying, then you pray. A way for her to become

more accustomed to praying is to keep a prayer and praise journal of prayer requests and answers. Use the Prayer and Praise Journal at the end of this book, or each of you can have a separate journal or notebook. When either of you has a prayer request or praise, write it in your journals; when you close in prayer, suggest she read aloud what she wrote. Soon she'll see that's praying!

2. *Pray Scripture.* Another way to pray is to personalize and pray Scripture. You can start with looking up the scriptural passages provided in each season's God's Perspective: Search the Scriptures Together, and personalize them as a prayer. For example, you could pray John 3:16 like this by filling in the blanks with your name:

> For God so loved me [_____] that he gave his only
> begotten son, Jesus, to die for me [_____] so that I
> [_____] will not perish. Thank you, Lord, for loving me
> so much. Amen.

3. *Ask questions.* Even though it's tempting to tell your mentee what she should do, scold her, or try to control her actions, those things are never effective. She might do what you say to please you, but her heart won't change. Your role is to help her learn to make right choices on her own. A good way to accomplish this is by asking questions. As she answers, she begins to see actions she should take or decisions to make, and then she takes ownership of her choices. The ultimate goal: she learns to rely on the Lord, not her mentor.

Kathy Collard Miller, a lay soul care counselor and mentor, uses the following questions to draw out the underlying reasons why a mentee has a hard time trusting God or to help her arrive at her own decisions or choices that would be pleasing to God. Kathy's book, *Never Ever Be the Same*, uses similar ideas to help readers trust God more.

1. What if you didn't keep doing that? What do you fear would happen?
2. What is God inviting you into through allowing these circumstances?
3. What would you like to say to that person who hurt you?
4. Why do you believe that's true when other people have told you it's not?
5. What were you hoping or longing for?
6. What do you feel is lacking in your life?
7. What does that choice provide for you?
8. What were you saying about yourself during the time that hurtful thing happened?
9. How does your behavior leave out God in your life?
10. How does that behavior protect you from some kind of harm or pain?
11. Everything is a choice. Why are you choosing that destructive behavior: to gain something or protect yourself from something?
12. What does your choice say about who God is?
13. What does your behavior or choice indicate regarding your beliefs about God, life, or other people?
14. What did the other person's reaction seem to say about you?

Pick questions applicable to the situation. Ask the questions conversationally—not as an interrogation—and give her time to respond. Don't guide her answers or expect her to arrive at the choices you want her to make. Always give her an opportunity to ask you questions.

Some Mentor Do's and Don'ts

Do's

- Pray together and share *your* prayer requests and praises.
- Set realistic goals for the relationship.

- Know your limits.
- Be a good listener.
- Set boundaries when and where needed.
- Be an encourager and nurture her to a closer relationship with God and his Word.
- Let her know you support her, but she is responsible for her choices.
- Keep everything you discuss in confidence, unless she gives you permission to share.
- Seek guidance from the Holy Spirit.
- Take the initiative in the relationship to keep it consistent and fresh.
- Take your Bible to every meeting and encourage her to bring hers.
- *Show* by example more than *telling* with words.
- Focus on what you give to the relationship, not what you expect to receive. A mentor is a servant for Christ—a reward in itself.

Don'ts

- Try to fix her situation, control the outcome, or make choices for her.
- Get in over your head. Seek outside and professional help for her if needed.
- Try to be her mother or best friend.
- Be critical or condemn, but don't condone sinful or harmful behavior.
- Feel like a failure if she makes bad choices or decisions. She's responsible before God.
- Make yourself available 24/7.
- Think your life has to be perfect. Let her see how you handle challenges.

- Talk to others about things she has shared. Trust is essential in mentoring relationships.[3]

Learning to Be a Vulnerable Mentor

In my "Feed my sheep" story I share in the Introduction, I mentioned mentoring my stepdaughter's young adult small group. Those young women didn't want to hear how good I was and how bad they were. They wanted honest vulnerability—sharing mistakes and identifying with their struggles and temptations. I gave my testimony of how life fell apart when I didn't follow Jesus, but when I rededicated my life to him, he turned my life around, and he would do the same for them.

This is often a hard lesson for a mentor to learn. They try to put on a perfect, got-it-all-together, Jesus-is-my-rock persona that no mentee thinks she could ever match. Or worse yet, she sees the mentor as fake because she knows no one's life is perfect and free of problems. No one remembers to turn to God *always*, even when we know we should.

Carrie Talbott learned that mentoring is vulnerability from the top down:

We were more than halfway through our nine months together as a group of seven in a "gap-year" ministry for college freshmen in Baja, Mexico—a perfect time to re-evaluate. Ministries can be breeding grounds for misunderstandings and hurt feelings, so at our meeting I gave everyone 3 by 5 cards. The purpose was twofold: write a few attaboys on one side and a few constructive criticisms on the other side, for each team member.

We swapped the cards. I naturally read the compliments first. The accolades boosted my confidence as a leader/mentor and confirmed feelings we previously exchanged in person. I liked them; they liked me. I flipped to the negative sides, not expecting anything too crushing.

There were little things I knew to improve, but the zinger came from our youngest female staff member: "I wish you were more vulnerable."

Like she wanted me to share dark secrets, confess failures, and admit weakness? Thanks, but no. And then *another* card: "When you never share any hardships in your life, it looks like you don't have any. I feel like I can't ever be as perfect as you."

Whoa there. Perfect? I hadn't shared much, but I was *so* far from perfect. Why would they think such things? On the inside, it was blatantly obvious to me I didn't have it all together. But on the outside, I had inadvertently conveyed exaggerated confidence.

These cards caught me off guard. I assumed our relationships were productive, lighthearted, and fun. Now, I clearly saw they had become one-sided. I regularly asked probing questions and gave examples of my past, but rarely gave examples of my present. Exactly what they longed for from me, an older woman—not old enough to be their mom—to come alongside in their journey. They wanted me to admit life wasn't blissful when God moved my family to another country, and how I felt guilty letting our kids watch another video while I attended meetings. Or how even after fifteen years, marriage was still hard.

I should have seen this coming, since I'm always looking for an older Christ-follower mentor who will share what makes her tick. How does she plan on serving in retirement? How has she gotten past her husband's idiosyncrasies? What does she consider a parenting flop and success? What kind of media does she take in and how does she avoid gossip? I don't care about her Facebook life. I'm talking about being in her home, watching how she builds up (or talks down to) her husband, how she treats telemarketers, and how she guards or flaps her tongue.

When I find women who make their lives look squeaky clean, I move on. I'm not interested in hearing about knickknack collections, extravagant vacations, new acquisitions, or neighborhood gossip. I want women offering kingdom-oriented meat and the fruit of the Spirit.

And younger women are looking for that in *my* generation too—the almost forties. Ladies who aren't afraid to be *real* role models and care more about obeying God than being politically or fashionably correct. I long to be authentic, but I'm learning that's impossible without vulnerability. When I find someone safe, I now try to practice being vulnerable. Not gigantic chunks . . . just little bits of my ugly. Small glimpses of my pride, selfishness, and jealousy. I hope to hear younger women say, "Oh, good—I thought I was the only one." And older women share things that make me say, "Oh, good—I thought I was the only one."

When Mentoring Is Hard

Mentoring for All Seasons has incredible stories of how mentoring changes and enhances the lives of M&M's, but what about the relationships that don't turn out so well? The mentee who ignores the mentor's wise counsel or flakes on their meetings? How does a mentor remain a good role model and not match the mentee's bad behavior?

I remind mentors that if the mentee had it all together, she'd be a mentor herself! A mentee needs accountability from someone who will challenge and prod her to become a godly woman in every season of life. The mentor stays a consistent godly woman, even when the mentee isn't responding appropriately—because that's what mentors do.

Resistant Mentee—*Renee Fisher*

I met Vickie when we were both students at Biola University—I was in my mid-twenties, and she was my mother's age. One day, I got discouraged and told Vickie I wanted to quit school. I didn't see how I could keep working and going to school full time. She told me to come over later that week and wait to make any major decisions until we talked. She suggested I write down my dreams on 3 by 5 cards: *everything* I enjoyed, strengths, future job ideas, and other.

When we met, I remember throwing the cards in front of her on the table and yelling, "THIS DOESN'T MAKE SENSE. There's no way I can continue working in a job I hate and going to school at night."

Vickie picked up my "Other" card, which had "Writing." She said I *had* to finish college because it would help with writing. It was as if she saw through my mess, picked up the card I least expected, and said what I needed to hear: College would help pursue my dreams of writing.

The next week, in the class that had made me want to quit school, the teacher asked if anyone had a blog. I was the only one with a blog. He pulled it up in front of the class and said, "You should publish these," referring to my devotionals.

Two years after graduating college, I published my first book, *Faithbook of Jesus*, and now I have nine published books. I hated Vickie's advice and didn't want to stay in school. If it weren't for Vickie lovingly speaking words of life over me, I might have quit and never followed through on my dream.

Persistent Mentor—*Rosalie*

When Monica introduced herself at the Woman to Woman Mentoring Orientation Coffee, she confessed she was a mess. I wondered who would be her mentor match. You guessed it; I was. We were both "older" women, although I like "mature."

When we first met, Monica had no trouble talking about the details of her complex family situation. She wanted to make necessary changes in her life, so we started setting goals. After a few weeks of meeting together, it became clear Monica had no safe boundaries.

As her finances dwindled, so did her health. At our weekly meetings, Monica made excuses and procrastinated on working at her goals. I offered tools to help work through her stressful circumstances:

1. A booklet to log weekly goals
2. A journal to write thoughts and concerns
3. Books on journaling and spiritual growth
4. *Becoming a Woman of Simplicity* by Cynthia Heald, which we selected to work on together
5. Scripture cards with verses on hope

As I prayed for wisdom in mentoring her, the Lord spoke to my heart about leading her gently to the Good Shepherd, Jesus, who would take care of all her needs. At our next meeting, we read Psalm 23, and I gave her Phillip Keller's *A Shepherd Looks at Psalm 23*. But my frustration increased each time we met: I couldn't motivate her to help herself. I took out my journal to write my thoughts and recorded the Lord's response:

Dear one,

This is not an easy task. Monica wants to lean on you.

*You need to lean on me for wisdom to advise her. She
will get through this mess with my grace. Call on me
together as your Good Shepherd. I will rescue her and
put her back on her feet. She is cast down. The weight of
responsibilities has overcome her. I want both of you to
focus on my presence each day so I may speak to your
hearts and comfort you. Encourage Monica to lean on me.*

I couldn't rescue Monica, but God could. I prompted
Monica to make time to be still and quiet before the Lord.
Since she couldn't do this at home, I suggested she go to
a park or coffee shop to find solitude. I urged her to take
her journal and Bible and call on the Lord. Ask for his
thoughts toward her and write them in her journal. I did
the same and made time to be still before the Lord. My role
as a mentor was to keep

- Praying she would work on her goals
- Praying for wisdom to guide her with God's grace
- Giving her scriptural verses of hope
- Standing by her through the storms

Toward the end of the six-month mentoring ministry
commitment, I prayed for more insight. The Lord assured
me I had taken Monica as far as I could. He had to take her
the rest of the way. It was up to her to turn her life over to
him and follow his lead. He could be the only one to walk
her through the victory trail.

God encouraged my heart while mentoring Monica.
Although I didn't see much change in her, *I saw a change in*

me. I had peace; I encouraged someone needing a friend. I listened. As a mentor, I grew spiritually. Working with a challenging person drew me closer to the Lord. I prayed often and sought God's wisdom more than I had before. I came through it stronger. "My grace is sufficient for you; for power is perfected in weakness" (2 Cor. 12:9 NASB). I text her occasionally, and slowly her mess is getting more manageable.

A Seeker Question and Salvation Prayer

Seeker Question: Are you ready to receive Jesus as your Savior, or are you going to reject him?

A Salvation Prayer (also use for rededication): Dear Jesus, I know I have sinned in my life, and I want to tell you how sorry I am. I ask you now to forgive me and cleanse me of those sins and help me to repent and stop sinning. Jesus, I want you to come into my heart and take residence there. I believe you are the Son of God who died on the cross to pay the price for my sins and then rose again in three days to offer me forgiveness and eternal life. Please fill me with the Holy Spirit and your love. Lord, I give you my life— make me a new creation in Christ. In Jesus's name, I pray. Amen.

Resources for Specific Seasons and Life Experiences

As you've seen from the stories in *Mentoring for All Seasons*, each mentoring relationship looks different, with different goals and outcomes. Here are some suggested books, Bible studies, websites, and resources for M&M's to learn more about mentoring or answer questions during a particular life season.

Seekers and New Believers
The Case for Christ by Lee Strobel
The Case for Christ Movie (available on DVD)
Why Do You Believe That? A Faith Conversation by Mary Jo Sharp
God's Not Dead Movie (available on DVD)

Tweens and Teens
Between Us Girls: Walks & Talks for Moms & Daughters by Trish Donohue
Raising a Modern-Day Princess by Pam Farrel and Doreen Hanna
Body. Beauty. Boys. The Truth about Girls & How We See Ourselves by
    Sarah Bragg
Totally God's: Every Girl's Guide to Faith, Friends, and Family by Megan
    Clinton and her dad, Dr. Tim Clinton
The Purity Code: God's Plan for Sex and Your Body by Jim Burns

Young Adults
Sex 180: There's More to It Than "Just Wait" by Chip Ingram and
    Tim Walker
Everyone Loves Sex, So Why Wait? by Bryan A. Sands
Boundaries in Dating: How Healthy Choices Grow Healthy Relationships by
    Henry Cloud and John Townsend
www.ratiochristi.org (a global movement that equips university students
    and faculty to give historical, philosophical, and scientific reasons for
    following Jesus Christ)

Marriage
Loving Your Husband by Cynthia Heald
The Power of a Praying Wife by Stormie Omartian
Men Are Like Waffles, Women Are Like Spaghetti by Bill and Pam Farrel
Why Can't He Be More Like Me?: 9 Secrets to Understanding Your Husband
    by Poppy Smith
*We All Married Idiots: Three Things You Will Never Change about Your
    Marriage and Ten Things You Can* by Elaine W. Miller

Singles
The 10 Best Decisions a Single Can Make: Embracing All God Has for You by
    Bill and Pam Farrel

Parenting

Unplanned Pregnancy
Deliver Me: Hope, Help, & Healing through True Stories of Unplanned Pregnancy by Dianne E. Butts

Mothering
The Making of a Mom by Stephanie Shott (www.themominitiative.com)
10 Secrets to Becoming a Worry-Free Mom by Cindi McMenamin
Mothering from Scratch by Melinda Means and Kathy Helgemo
Total Family Makeover: Practical Steps to Making Disciples at Home by Melissa Spoelstra
31 Days to Becoming a Happy Mom by Arlene Pellicane

Mothering Special Needs Children and Children with Illnesses
Hope for Families of Children on the Autistic Spectrum by Lynda T. Young
Hope for Families of Children with Cancer by Lynda T. Young and Chaplain Johnathan Ward
Josiah's Fire: Autism Stole His Words. God Gave Him a Voice by Tahni Cullen and Cheryl Ricker
Refresh: Spiritual Nourishment for Parents of Children with Special Needs by Kimberly M. Drew and Jocelyn Green

Mothering Prodigals
Praying for Your Prodigal Daughter: Hope, Help, & Encouragement for Hurting Parents by Janet Thompson (discussion questions; book can also apply to sons)
Messy Journey: How Grace and Truth Offer the Prodigal a Way Home by Lori Wildenberg

Stepmoms
101 Tips for the Smart Stepmom by Laura Petherbridge (www.TheSmartStepmom.com)

Illness and Health Issues
Dear God, They Say It's Cancer: A Companion Guide for Women on the Breast Cancer Journey by Janet Thompson

"The Top Thirteen Things *to Do* or Say and *Not to Do* or Say to Someone
with Breast Cancer" (www.womantowomanmentoring.com/support
/breast-cancer/)

Infertility
*Dear God, Why Can't I Have a Baby? A Companion Guide for Couples on
the Infertility Journey* by Janet Thompson
"The Top Fifteen Things *Not* to Say or Do and *To* Say or Do to Someone
Experiencing Infertility" and "Suggested Responses" (www
.womantowomanmentoring.com/support/infertility)

Gender Identity Issues, Sexual Integrity, and Recovery from Sexual Abuse
What Do I Say to a Friend Who's Gay? by Emily Parke Chase
Loves God, Likes Girls: A Memoir by Sally Gary
The Armor of God by Priscilla Shirer (a study on spiritual warfare)
The Wounded Heart by Dan Allender (for sexual abuse victims
and survivors)
www.exodusglobalalliance.org/index.php (Exodus Global Alliance—
helping people with same-sex attractions)
www.desertstream.org (Desert Stream Ministries—Christ-centered help
for those struggling with sexual and relational problems)
www.celebraterecovery.com (Celebrate Recovery—a Christ-centered
recovery program in churches)
www.joedallas.com (Genesis Counseling—counseling for Christians
struggling with sexual integrity, including spouses of sexual addicts)
www.purelifeministries.org (Pure Life Ministries—for Christians dealing
with sexual sin with the goal of leading Christians to victory over
sexual sin through a deeper life in God)

Post-Abortion Recovery
Surrendering the Secret: Healing the Heartbreak of Abortion by Patricia
Layton
www.rachelsvineyard.org (Rachel's Vineyard—a post-abortion retreat)
www.silentnomoreawareness.org (Silent No More—resources for finding
abortion healing help)

Tragedy
Waiting for Heaven: Finding Beauty in the Pain and the Struggle by
  Heather Gillis

Caregiving
JOY-spirations for Caregivers by Annetta Dellinger and Karen Boerger

Midlife and Grandparenting
10 Secrets of Living Smart, Savvy, and Strong by Pam Farrel
I'm Too Young to Be This Old by Poppy Smith
Grandparenting with a Purpose by Lillian Penner
  (www.christiangrandparenting.net)
*Grandparenting through Obstacles: Overcoming Family Challenges to
  Reach Your Grandchildren for Christ* by Dianne E. Butts and
  Renne Gray-Wilburn

Retiring and Downsizing
Dear God, He's Home!: A Woman's Guide to Her Stay-at-Home Man by
  Janet Thompson

Mentoring Memoir
Dolores, Like the River by Laura L. Padgett

Biblical Guide to Answering Questions about Issues Women Face Today
God is My Strength: Fifty Biblical Responses to Issues Facing Women Today
  by Patricia A. Ennis

Mentoring Resources by Janet Thompson
Bible Studies for M&M's to Do Together
Face-to-Face with Mary and Martha: Sisters in Christ
Face-to-Face with Naomi and Ruth: Together for the Journey
Face-to-Face with Elizabeth and Mary: Generation to Generation
Face-to-Face with Priscilla and Aquila: Balancing Life and Ministry
Face-to-Face with Euodia and Syntyche: From Conflict to Community
Face-to-Face with Sarah, Rachel, and Hannah: Pleading with God
Face-to-Face with Lois and Eunice: Nurturing Faith in Your Family

Mentoring in a World Forsaking God

*Forsaken God?: Remembering the Goodness of God Our Culture Has
Forgotten* by Janet Thompson (Discussion questions)

Starting a Woman to Woman Mentoring Ministry

Available exclusively at www.womantowomanmentoring.com
/publications/woman-to-woman-mentoring-resources

*Woman to Woman Mentoring: How to Start, Grow, and Maintain a
Mentoring Ministry DVD Leader Kit*

Woman to Woman Mentoring Ministry Coordinator's Guide

Woman to Woman Mentoring Training Leader's Guide

Woman to Woman Mentoring Mentor and Mentee Handbooks

Locating Scripture Verses

You don't have to know the exact scriptural reference. If you have
an idea of what it says or can think of a couple of words in the
verse, you can go to a website like www.biblegateway.com or www
.blueletterbible.com and put in the word or phrase, and the site will
bring up all the verses with that word or phrase. That's how I found
many of the scriptural passages to use in this book. You can also use
the concordance in the back of many Bibles or an online Bible.

PRAYER & PRAISE JOURNAL

Prayer Request	Praises

PRAYER & PRAISE JOURNAL

Prayer Request	Praises

PRAYER & PRAISE JOURNAL

Prayer Request	Praises

PRAYER & PRAISE JOURNAL

Prayer Request	Praises

PRAYER & PRAISE JOURNAL

Prayer Request	Praises

PRAYER & PRAISE JOURNAL

Prayer Request	Praises

GUIDE FOR USING *MENTORING FOR ALL SEASONS* IN MENTORING RELATIONSHIPS, BIBLE STUDY/SMALL GROUPS, AND BOOK CLUBS

Mentoring for All Seasons is perfect to read and study together as M&M's in a mentoring relationship or in a group setting such as a book club, Bible study, or women's small group or life group, especially if you have a mentoring ministry at your church or are considering starting one. Read a chapter, or portion of a chapter, between meetings; discuss the "Let's Talk about It" discussion questions when you get together. I've provided a sample format below for group meetings. Select a discussion leader or rotate that privilege. The leader keeps the group on track and conversation flowing.

Guidelines for a Book Club or Bible Study/ Small Group

- Don't share personal information that would make you or someone else uncomfortable.
- Everything personal discussed in the group stays in the group.
- Make sure everyone has an opportunity to share and that one person doesn't dominate.
- This isn't a counseling session. It's okay to give tips and suggestions that have worked for you, but don't try to "fix" another person's situation.

- Prayer requests stay within the group unless the person concerned has given permission to ask others for prayer.

Suggested Group Format

- Open in prayer.
- Discuss and answer questions from the Let's Talk about It section of the chapter you've read.
- Ask each participant to name one or more things she gained from this chapter and how she will apply it to her life.
- Have general discussion.
- Share prayer requests.
- Enjoy fellowship.

ABOUT HIS WORK MINISTRIES

About His Work Ministries is Janet Thompson's writing and speaking ministry. Janet has an MBA from California Lutheran University and an MA in Christian Leadership from Fuller Theological Seminary. Through her authored resources, *Woman to Woman Mentoring: How to Start, Grow, and Maintain a Mentoring Ministry* and *Face-to-Face Bible Study* series, thousands of women around the world enjoy the blessings and rewards of mentoring. Janet's passion is to equip men and women to practice Titus 2:1–8 and mentor the next generation in a lifestyle pleasing to God.

Janet is also the author of the following publications:

- *Forsaken God?: Remembering the Goodness of God Our Culture Has Forgotten*
- *The Team That Jesus Built: How to Develop, Equip, and Commission a Women's Ministry Team*
- *Dear God, They Say It's Cancer: A Companion Guide for Women on the Breast Cancer Journey*
- *Dear God, Why Can't I Have a Baby? A Companion Guide for Couples on the Infertility Journey*
- *Dear God, He's Home!: A Woman's Guide to Her Stay-at-Home Man*

- *Praying for Your Prodigal Daughter: Hope, Help &
Encouragement for Hurting Parents*
- *God's Best for Your Life*

For More Information and to Contact Janet

Janet Thompson
About His Work Ministries
Conference, event, and retreat speaking
Mentoring, training, and coaching aspiring writers and
ministry leaders

Freelance author and editor
Email: info@womantowomanmentoring.com
www.womantowomanmentoring.com
twitter.com/AHWministries
facebook.com/janetthompson.authorspeaker
pinterest.com/thompsonjanet

NOTES

Preface
[1]Tracy Steel, "Oaks of Righteousness—Mentors Matter Monday," *Ruth's Hope,* April 1, 2013, http://www.ruthshope.org/oaks-of-righteousness-mentors-matter-monday. Adapted with permission.

Introduction
[1]Klaus Issler, *Wasting Time with God* (Downers Grove: InterVarsity Press, 2001), 180.

Chapter 1
[1]Karen Trigg, Introduction to "In the Corner—Like A Wallflower—Mentors Matter Monday," *Ruth's Hope,* March 11, 2013, www.ruthshope.org/in-the-corner-like-a-wallflower. Adapted with permission.

[2]Issler, *Wasting Time with God,* 180.

Chapter 2
[1]Tina Wilson, "In the Corner—Like A Wallflower—Mentors Matter Monday," *Ruth's Hope,* March 11, 2013, http://www.ruthshope.org/in-the-corner-like-a-wallflower. Adapted with permission.

Chapter 3
[1]Missy Robertson, "Mentorship," January 25, 2016, http://tinyurl.com/z3hmr3h.

[2]Tracey Crum, "Nothing More Confusing—Mentors Matter Monday" *Ruth's Hope,* December 6, 2012, http://www.ruthshope.org/nothing-more-confusing-guest-post. Adapted with permission.

Chapter 5
[1]Sharon Jaynes, *Take Hold of the Faith You Long For: Let Go, Move Forward, Live Bold* (Grand Rapids, MI: Baker Books, 2016), 32.

[2]Sharon Jaynes, "When Your Heart Longs for Something More," Proverbs 31 Ministries, May 2, 2016, http://proverbs31.org/devotions/devo/when-your-heart-longs-for-something-more/.

Chapter 6
[1]Lucibel Van Atta, *Women Encouraging Women* (Sisters: Multnomah, 1987), 28 (out of print).

Section 2
[1]Keith R. Anderson and Randy D. Reese, *Spiritual Mentoring* (Downers Grove: InterVarsity, 1999), 38.

Chapter 7
[1]Oswald Chambers, *My Utmost for His Highest,* updated edition. James Reimann, ed. (Grand Rapids: Discovery House, 1995).

Chapter 8
[1]Pam Farrel and Doreen Hanna, *Raising a Modern-Day Princess* (Carol Stream: Tyndale House, 2009), 22.

[2]Janet Thompson, *Face-to-Face with Elizabeth and Mary: Generation to Generation* (Birmingham: New Hope, 2010), 15.

[3]Owen Strachan, "What the Future Holds," *Tabletalk Magazine*, August 2015, 22.

Chapter 9
[1]Scott McConnell, "LifeWay Research Finds Reasons 18- to 22-Year-Olds Drop Out of Church," August 7, 2007, http://tinyurl.com/3ulgtkx.

Chapter 10
[1]"Quotes on Marriage, from Billy and Ruth Bell Graham," https://quotecloset.wordpress.com/2013/02/04/quotes-on-marriage-from-billy-and-ruth-bell-graham.

Chapter 12
[1]Susan Yates, "The Seasons of Motherhood: Recognizing, Challenges, Focusing on Blessings," *Family Life*, 2016, http://tinyurl.com/h2gskea.

[2]"11 Facts about Teen Pregnancy," DoSomething.org, https://www.dosomething.org/us/facts/11-facts-about-teen-pregnancy.

[3]*Finding Mommy Bliss* © 2014 by Genny Heikka. Story appears courtesy of Hallway Publishing.

Chapter 13
[1]Janet Thompson, *Dear God, Why Can't I Have a Baby?* (Abilene: Leafwood), 122.

[2]Glenn T. Stanton, "5 Reasons Target's Trans Bathroom Policy Really Stepped In It," *The Federalist*, April 29, 2016, http://preview.tinyurl.com/gpec2k4.

[3]"Being Transgender Is Not a Mental Disorder," *Time Magazine,* August 8, 2016, 21.

[4] Sally Gary, *Loves God, Likes Girls: A Memoir* (Abilene: Leafwood, 2013), 236–237.

[5] Ashley Chesnut, "The Church's Modern Scarlet Letter," LifeWay Women's Ministry, August 29, 2016, http://tinyurl.com/hwlw9df. Adapted with permission.

Epilogue

[1] Rhonda H. Kelly, "JoAnn Leavell: My Mentor and Me," March 6, 2015, https://talkingisagift.files.wordpress.com/2015/03/joann-leavell-my-mentor-and-me.pdf. Adapted with permission.

Appendix

[1] © 2016 Kara Tippetts. *And It Was Beautiful,* published by David C Cook. All rights reserved.

[2] Karen Trigg, "Who—Me? She's Asking Me to Mentor Her," *Ruth's Hope,* http://www.ruthshope.org/freebies/who-me-shes-asking-me-to-mentor-her. Adapted with permission.

[3.] Adapted from Janet Thompson, *Woman to Woman Mentoring: Mentor Handbook* (Garden Valley: AHW Publishing, 2000), 20.